1981

Londonwalks

This series originated with
PARISWALKS *by Alison and Sonia Landes*. Other titles in the
series include:

JERUSALEMWALKS *by Nitza Rosovsky*
FLORENCEWALKS *by Anne Holler* (forthcoming)

ANTON POWELL

Londonwalks

Photographs by Robin Laurance

An Owl Book
A New Republic Book
Henry Holt and Company
New York

Copyright © 1981 by Anton Powell
Photographs copyright © 1981 by Robin Laurance
All rights reserved, including the right to reproduce this
book or portions thereof in any form.

Published by Henry Holt and Company, Inc., 521
Fifth Avenue, New York, New York 10175.

Distributed in Canada by Fitzhenry & Whiteside
Limited, 195 Allstate Parkway, Markham,
Ontario L3R 4T8.

Library of Congress Cataloging in Publication Data
Powell, Anton.
Londonwalks.
"A New republic book."
Includes index.
1. London—Description—1951–   —Tours. I. Title.
DA679.P68   914.21′04858   81-632 AACR1
ISBN 0-8050-0552-8 (An Owl Book)

Designer: Jacqueline Schuman
Maps by David Lindroth
Printed in the United States of America
7 9 10 8 6

ISBN 0-8050-0552-8

Contents

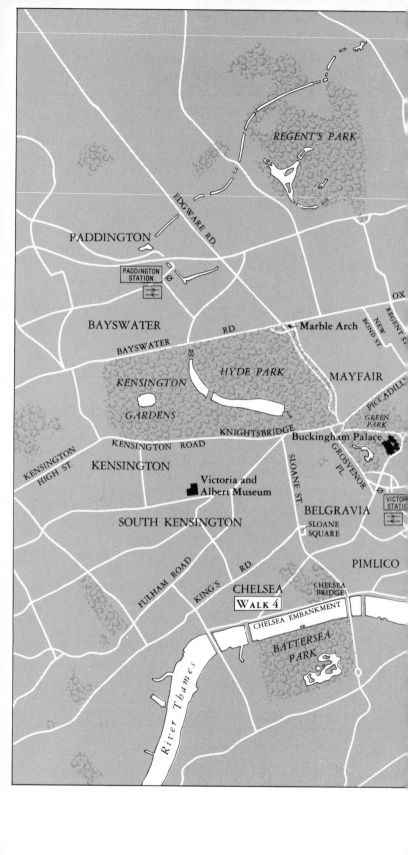

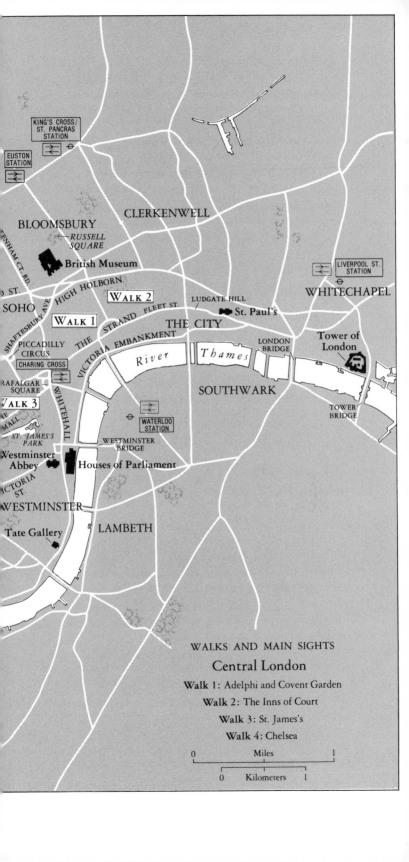

KING'S CROSS/
ST. PANCRAS
STATION

EUSTON
STATION

BLOOMSBURY

CLERKENWELL

RUSSELL
SQUARE

British Museum

TENHAM CT. RD.

HIGH HOLBORN

WALK 2

O ST.

SOHO

SHAFTESBURY AVE

WALK 1

THE STRAND

FLEET ST.

LUDGATE HILL

LIVERPOOL ST.
STATION

WHITECHAPEL

St. Paul's

THE CITY

Tower of
London

PICCADILLY
CIRCUS

CHARING CROSS

THE

VICTORIA EMBANKMENT

River

Thames

LONDON
BRIDGE

AFALGAR
SQUARE

WALK 3

MALL

WHITEHALL

WATERLOO
STATION

SOUTHWARK

TOWER
BRIDGE

ST. JAMES'S
PARK

WESTMINSTER
BRIDGE

Westminster
Abbey

Houses of Parliament

CTORIA
ST.

WESTMINSTER

LAMBETH

Tate Gallery

WALKS AND MAIN SIGHTS

Central London

Walk 1: Adelphi and Covent Garden

Walk 2: The Inns of Court

Walk 3: St. James's

Walk 4: Chelsea

0   Miles   1

0   Kilometers   1

Acknowledgments

Although there were many people who helped me, there is space to mention only a few. Dr. Sarah Potter read the whole of my manuscript patiently, promptly and with a scholarly eye. Jane Fallis contributed important improvements to its style. Alan Myers gave professional help on points of law, and Dr. David Tucker advised on the subject of Dickens. Pam Wierengo and Madge Caro put their wide knowledge of Chelsea at my disposal. Tony Sympson told me about the history of Goodwin's Court, the seventeenth-century street which he and his family have preserved. Holly Brennan gave efficient and courteous help in the Chelsea Public Library.

Almost every writer on London's history is, or ought to be, deeply indebted to the many-volumed *Survey of London*, now published by the Greater London Council. After inspecting the often fanciful works of local historians, I found it a frequent pleasure and relief to turn to the *Survey,* with its meticulous attention to sources. Also valuable were Thea Holme's *Chelsea* and Kellow Chesney's magnificent book *The Victorian Underworld*—a factual guide to the seedy glamour of Dickens's London.

I owe an unusual debt to Susan and Julia Poate, who first aroused my interest in London. Friends in the American media to whom I have special reason for gratitude are R. W. Apple, Jr., William A. Davis and Rod MacLeish. Ian McCannah of the organization London Walks has given support in innumerable ways.

Finally, my thanks to the patient editors at New Republic Books, Joan Tapper, who began the editing of this book, and Marc Granetz, who finished it.

Londonwalks

Introduction

This book aims to show you places that visitors rarely find, and which British people themselves often know little about. Most of London is still undiscovered. There are pubs gleaming with Victorian mahogany and etched glass that have no signs to inform you of their age. In Covent Garden, one of the areas we shall visit, whole streets are still lit by nineteenth-century gaslights, yet no one pays them much attention—the local people don't notice because the lights are perfectly efficient (that is why they're still there); and visitors usually don't see them because most of Covent Garden, like all the districts we shall look at, is off the well-traveled tourist routes.

I've tried to make this book a "good read" for home or hotel, and also an accurate guide on the ground. It contains four walks, each taking about 2½ hours, a pace which allows you to look at places in proper detail—at metal cones by house doors used for putting out torches in the eighteenth century, at tiny windows barred against nineteenth-century child thieves, at forgotten courtyards and at specialty, sometimes eccentric, businesses.

London has to be discovered on foot. Trying to learn about it from a tourist bus or a car would be rather like trying to learn about the United States from a plane. The views would be interesting and often magnificent, but it would be hard to find out much about the people and their history.

Guidebooks, even some of the best, can be superficial if they try to cover huge areas of the city. Here is an example:

> The narrow St. James's Place, opening on the west here, has a variety of pleasant old houses. Spencer House, on the left facing Green Park, is a large mansion in a classical style built in 1765 by John Vardy and restored in 1957 after war damage. No. 26, next to it, is a distinctive block of flats [apartments] by Denys Lasdun (1959).

Just three sentences for a fascinating seventeeth-century street that we shall be visiting. It was the street

1

where, in the 1660s, a powerful royal mistress had an elaborate underground "freezer" for wine; where, in the 1820s, the artist who did the original and outrageous "Tom and Jerry" cartoons lived; and where you can also see the splendid, gaslit home of a famous politician who came to a tragic end in 1830. A street like this needs, and will get, pages to itself.

To help you find the places along the walks, I have often used measurement in yards ("Ten yards farther, on the left. . ."). By a yard I mean just a longish stride. I hope this method is less frustrating than the more traditional guidebook vocabulary of "nearby" and "farther down the street." After a while you will know whether my paces are shorter or longer than yours, and you can make the necessary adjustments.

Information and Advice

First Impressions

In almost any foreign country some things are better, some worse, than at home. On the first days of a vacation it's easy to be either starry-eyed or unreasonably depressed. But you will soon notice trade-offs. In England, pubs, theaters and public transport are a big plus; restaurants less so. The public discipline of the British in forming queues (lines) on the pavement (sidewalk) is often admired, but their indiscipline on the roads is sometimes frightening. You will find, too, that the British think *they* are the ones who speak English—there's an old line about England and America being divided by a common language—even though Americans often come closer to reproducing the English of Shakespeare's day. There is a selected glossary of differences between the American and British dialects later in this chapter. Young people's slang in Britain is largely American in origin, but you may find older people's slang less familiar. For instance, to the young the police are often "fuzz" and sometimes even "Feds," even though Britain has no FBI and is not a federation. For older folk the police can be "rozzers" or "Old Bill." The word "bobbies" is now genteel, dated and rarely used.

British dress differs slightly from American. Women wear fewer slacks, raincoats and head scarves than in the States. Men's trousers are less colorful and are longer in the leg, and belts are less in evidence.

Feminism is less strong in Britain than in the States, and the women's groups that do exist are often dominated by Americans. On the streets, in advertisements and on British TV you will see more female flesh than in America. The British also tolerate more off-color jokes. America has inherited the Puritan tradition of the emigré Pilgrim Fathers. Remember that the British are descended from the folks who stayed behind.

In Britain, as in much of Europe, safety in public is taken for granted and rarely mentioned. I can't remember ever having heard a British male say that there was somewhere in Britain he wouldn't walk. Unaccompanied women are more careful, though most will walk almost anywhere at any time. Purse-snatching is uncommon in the street, except for two or three areas far from the center of London and also a long way from the districts described in this book. But it's worth guarding against purse-thieves on tube platforms; they operate just as the train doors are closing, and distract their victim by jostling her while rifling her purse.

If you go outside London, two points: people walk and perform business transactions more slowly. Second, almost all private farmland is treated as common land, with many "public footpaths" for walking and picnicking. Keep a respectful distance from farm buildings, walk around crops rather than through them, and leave gates as you find them (open or closed). Otherwise, don't be inhibited; for the discreet visitor the British countryside is one great park. Farmers, if you meet them, may well be flattered to have visitors from abroad.

Transportation

From Heathrow Airport, think twice about taking a taxi: the cost is high. The underground ("tube" or "underground"—never "subway," which is an underground pedestrian walkway) now connects the airport to central London and most points around the city, and trains leave every few minutes. If you do take a taxi, tell the driver your destination and ask for an estimate of the price before getting in. The driver will probably tell you that the cost of the journey is determined by his meter, but he (usually it's a he) knows roughly what it will be. Settling this beforehand may just save you from an unwanted circular tour. Don't show the driver a map. It probably won't tell him anything about London but it may tell him something about you. Also remember that a taxi's territory is the entire city, and you can't be refused because your destination might be inconvenient. If you have any problems, every taxi has an identification number on the back of the driver's seat; taxi licenses are difficult to come by and most drivers don't want trouble—and won't start it. Except for rare occurrences at airports and other such spots, London taxi drivers on the whole are far more courteous and more knowledgeable about the streets than taxi drivers in most major cities around the world. In central London taxis are often a good value, especially if you have two or three friends with you (the extra cost per person is very small). The taxis to use, if at all possible, are the tall black Austins. Their yellow signs are illuminated when the taxi is available for hire. Unmarked taxis (usually called "minicabs," whatever their size) don't have meters, and the driver charges what he thinks he can get; so it's vital to agree on a price in advance.

Nearly all the public buses in London are the red double-deckers, and from the upper deck you will get some pleasant views. The top deck is also the smoking section. Buses are cheaper than the underground because the service is slower and less reliable. If you are in a hurry, don't trust a bus. (Also remember to queue for the bus; frequently one will pull up and the ticket-taker will say, "One on top, two inside," and only the first three people in the queue can board.) But for a romantic, rumbling journey through London on a sunny day, buses are unbeatable. The no. 137 bus, for instance, will take you through the main shopping district (the West End), past Chelsea, across the Thames, through working-class Battersea and out to the wooded parklands on the southern fringe of London—all for a very low fare. Maps of the bus routes and the underground system are free at tourist bureaus and many underground stations.

The underground is London's main transportation system; it runs from about 6:00 A.M. until midnight. It is noisy, safe and unromantic—without the frills or rubber wheels of the Paris *métro*. It's also expensive in comparison with other metro systems. London Transport, which runs the buses and tubes, urges visitors to buy "Go as You Please" tickets, which serve for all bus and tube journeys. Beware of these tickets; they are very highly priced to make sure that cunning commuters don't use them for daily journeys the length of London. If you are planning any sort of routine—like a regular evening journey between a hotel and theater-land—you will probably get much better value from a weekly season ticket between two stations of your choice. This ticket, which can be bought at any station, will also count towards the cost of journeys farther afield.

Driving in Britain is dangerous and undisciplined compared with the United States. Speed limits—30 mph in town, 70 on motorways and elsewhere—are broken as a matter of course, and drivers change lanes with little or no warning. An American friend, watching with amused horror as a mob of European cars cut across one another, told me, "If you did that in the States, they wouldn't give you a ticket—they'd put you in the clink!" (As an Englishman, my first experience of American roads was one of relief—that I'd escaped from the amateur racetrack of London streets.) Parking space is hard to find in London, and even residents often find that public transportation is not only cheaper than using a car, but also quicker.

Hotels

Hotels are often more expensive than in the United States, especially when ultramodern. Shared bathrooms are usual (you pay a good deal more for a private bath), and it is unusual to have a television in your room. Don't despise the hotels in Victorian buildings; they are usually cheaper, the service is often good and the buildings themselves have more character. To British thinking, there is nothing unfashionable about staying in an old hotel; in fact the most chic hotels are rarely modern. West London (around South Kensington and Earl's Court) has many hotels and is much used by visitors. This seems to me a great pity; the area is noisy and restless, and it has prices aimed at the inexperienced visitor. Even the British population here is transient and exploited: secretaries living beyond their means and young accountants shoehorned into partitioned bedrooms. West London may be slightly reassuring, because closer to Heathrow Airport, but I would strongly recommend visitors to look for a hotel in the Russell Square/Bloomsbury area, just to the northeast of central London.

There are large modern hotels close to Russell Square tube station (which is on a direct line to the airport) and smaller hotels in elegant nineteenth-century buildings nearby in the streets by the British Museum (especially in Montague Street and Bedford Place).

This district is quieter and cheaper than West London, with older and more attractive buildings. The streets just south of the British Museum have small and slightly bohemian shops and cafés, frequented by museum visitors and staff. Theater-land (around Covent Garden), the main restaurant areas (Soho and Covent Garden) and the chief shopping district (Oxford Street) are all within walking distance. The Russell Square/ Bloomsbury area is also handy for three of the four walks in this book.

England is famous for its "bed & breakfast" accommodations (b & b's). In the countryside this means quiet, comfortable rooms in someone's house plus a large English breakfast in the morning, and occasionally before-bed tea. But in London most places that advertise themselves as "b & b's" are really just inexpensive large hotels with little, if any, real personalized hospitality, and a continental breakfast (coffee or tea and a roll with jam), not an English one.

Restaurants and Shops

London has a cosmopolitan population and for that reason you'll find a huge range of ethnic restaurants. I have included a list of recommended restaurants at the end of the book. Over the years I have been most impressed by three—one Spanish, one Greek Cypriot and one Nepalese. In general the British are fond of Chinese, Greek Cypriot and Indian food; all three kinds are moderately priced. The Chinese dishes and Indian curries are usually hotter than those served in the United States. In an Indian restaurant ask for a mild curry, and be prepared to order yogurt to add to it if you still find it too hot. Good Chinese restaurants cluster in and around Gerrard Street in Soho; a Chinese friend tells me that it's called simply "China Street" by the Chinese themselves. In almost all restaurants you will have to ask for water; iced water is not generally served.

In British restaurants and shops the consumer does not rule. Customers are often timid, shop assistants and waiters often aloof. The class system is probably at work here; until quite recently the upper class expected deference from staff, who responded by becoming snobs themselves and treating poorer customers accordingly. Waiters and salespeople either dominate or are dominated; there is little democracy. (British people who cross the Atlantic often get a pleasant surprise when they find that American staff regard being friendly as part of the job.) Service in Britain will probably improve if staff pay is drastically increased. Traditionally, shop assistants and waiters are badly paid even by British standards. Consumers themselves are slow to make a fuss, fearing to attract attention and be shown up. The British generally are shy; "I was so embarrassed" is one of the commonest phrases in conversation.

In restaurants, look at the foot of the bill of fare, to see not just whether the service charge is included, but also whether the prices include the (hated) Value Added Tax—generally referred to as "V.A.T." or "vat". This varies in amount from year to year, but can be as high as 15 percent.

Tipping

For taxi drivers, 10 to 15 percent; 10 to 15 percent for restaurants with no fixed service charge—unless the service has been poor. A couple of silver coins for hotel porters. Don't tip theater or cinema attendants unless they've done something very special for you. In greasy-spoon cafés and fish-and-chip shops tips aren't expected, and sometimes the staff won't know how to react if you offer one. In an eating place, a rough guide as to when to tip is: yes, if there's a tablecloth. But there are a few Formica-top-table places which do give restaurant service and where tips are expected.

Shopping

The best-known shopping district, Oxford Street, has a branch of the highly reputable Marks and Spencer's (good for clothes). The other very large stores in Oxford Street give reasonable value, but the small shops here have prices aimed at the inexperienced visitor. More interesting are the shops in Covent Garden (reasonable value) and Jermyn Street (expensive), which are mentioned in our first and third walks. Both areas are good for gifts. For inexpensive fresh food, Chapel Market (near Angel tube station) with its open-air stalls is outstanding; it also has a branch of Sainsbury's, Britain's most respected food chain. Middlesex Street ("Petticoat Lane"), close to Liverpool Street tube station, has a famous open-air clothes market on Sunday mornings. It's good for people-watching and for listening to the cheery backchat of the stall-holders, but bargains are few. Look for them instead in the neighboring side streets between Middlesex Street and Brick Lane. For interesting junk and secondhand clothes, Portobello Road (Ladbroke Grove tube station) has a good street market on Saturdays and is popular with young people, who come carefully dressed in the penniless-chic style. Street markets are some of the liveliest and most cheerful places in London; look out, though, for the modern practitioners of the Dickensian tradition of "dipping" (picking pockets). For the addresses of shops and museums, don't forget that London's most useful book is the telephone directory.

Pubs

Here London excels, the pubs often being works of art in themselves with their elaborate plaster ceilings, woodwork and mirrors. The atmosphere is usually relaxed and democratic, and unaccompanied women go in as a matter of course. There used to be a protocol in pubs that kept locals and the lower classes in a "Public Bar" area, middle and upper classes in a "Private Bar" area, and men and women together in a "Saloon Bar." These distinctions don't mean much today (especially in central London) but some signs for them still exist, and there are certain neighborhood pubs where these and other protocols are followed to some extent (some interesting Cockney pubs of Southwark among them, but mostly out in the country—where, by and large, the best, most atmospheric pubs are). Pubs are not recognized pickup places; singles bars are virtually unknown in Britain. Heavy drinking is unusual; far more often, pubs are used for making business deals or for spending an evening with friends. Prices in central London pubs vary only slightly; if a Londoner says that a pub is expensive, all that's meant is that beer is a few pence more per pint than elsewhere.

Beer generally is served by gas pressure and, apart

from lager, is darker and sweeter than most American brews. Since the early 1970s gassed beer has been the target of one of Britain's very few consumer revolts—the Campaign for Real Ale. The beer served by use of carbon dioxide is biochemically dead, usually short on alcohol, and needs little or no skill to serve. The big brewing corporations, which own most pubs, adopted it soon after the Second World War, claiming that bar staff were incapable of serving the traditional beer properly. Traditional beer (Real Ale) is flat, contains living yeast, is often strong and is served by hand pump after maturing in the pub's cellar. The Campaign for Real Ale, made up largely of young middle-class men, attacks the Big Bad Brewers and champions the small companies that have persevered with traditional beer. In London it has been highly successful, forcing the big corporations to remove some of their plastic-pump displays and fizzy beer and to replace them with the vertical hand pumps and Real Ale. The most re-spected brewery in London is the small firm of Young's, which produces consistently excellent Real Ale from a brewery in a South London farmyard. Much of it is then delivered by horse-drawn wagon.

All English pubs are closed by law in the afternoon; in London closing time is 3:00 P.M. (2:00 on Sunday), reopening at 5:30 (7:00 on Sunday). Evening closing is at 10:30 or 11:00. These often annoying restrictions have resulted from governmental attempts to prevent drunkenness among munitions workers during the First World War.

Cinemas

The large cinemas show mainly the latest popular films from America. But scattered around London is a rich variety of classic, avant-garde and foreign-language films. Tracking them down, often in unfamiliar parts of London and sometimes late at night, is a favorite adventure of Londoners themselves. For details of programs, see "Entertainments" below. Especially good, and easily reached, is the Academy Cinema in Oxford Street, which usually shows excellent European films. A film's being shown at the Academy is a recommendation in itself.

Entertainments

The best general guide is a weekly magazine called *What's On*. The magazine *Time Out* is similar, but has an uneasy editorial mixture of trendiness and radicalism and is written in a mid-Atlantic style. *Time Out* is, however, especially good for details of foreign-language and avant-garde films.

Newspapers

Perhaps the best guide to England's news publications is the following well-known, pithy characterization.

"The *Financial Times* is read by the people who own the country; the *Times* by the people who run the country. The *Daily Mail* is read by the wives of the people who run the country; the *Guardian* by liberals who *think* they run the country. The *Daily Telegraph* is read by the people who used to run the country [ex-officers, elderly aristocrats]; the *Daily Express* by people who want the Queen to run the country. The *Daily Mirror* is read by people who want the unions to run the country; the [Communist] *Morning Star* is read by people who want another country to run the country; the [mildly pornographic] *Sun* is read by people who don't care who runs the country so long as she has big tits."

There's also the magazine *Private Eye*, a bold mixture of esoteric satire and straight exposé.

Asking for Information

In choosing local people to approach for information, look for someone who doesn't seem in a hurry. A working-class person of fifty or older is often a good bet, because he or she may well have lived in the area for many years. "Working class" in Britain does not mean "poor"; most of the population is working class. A working-class person, roughly speaking, is someone who does a non-professional job, has a local accent and does not have a college education. One of the best-informed Londoners I have met was an elderly porter, sitting on a fruit barrow amid the picturesque grime of Whitechapel. Working-class men like this may take pride, patronizing but friendly, in answering your questions. The women, in my experience, know just as much but are more modest and also have a nicer sense of humor. On a bus I once overheard two working-class, middle-aged London women talking about marriage and True Love. "Well," said one of them with resigned cheerfulness, "I don't know about True Love, but he'll be lucky to find another old donkey to work for him like I have!" If you ask for information from a group of women in a street market or a party of women office workers, you may well find yourself getting advice and good-humored jokes for several minutes.

Help

Visitors who are seriously injured or contract infectious diseases can get free treatment under the National Health Service when taken to the casualty department of a hospital. (Until October 1981 free

treatment was not so restricted; this change in policy requires visitors to see to their travel insurance needs before arriving.) Not every hospital has a casualty department; of those that do, University College Hospital (Gower Street, WC1, tel. 387-9300) has a fine reputation.

A neighborhood doctor will also treat you free of charge (private medicine is used only by the minority in Britain). Patients are usually seen in the morning at about 9:00 and again in the late afternoon. (Exact times are advertised outside the clinics or houses where doctors practice. Office hours are called "surgery hours.") Boots, a large drugstore at Piccadilly Circus, fills prescriptions from 8:30 A.M. to 8:00 P.M. (Drugstores are called "chemists"; those that fill prescriptions are called "dispensing chemists.") The three emergency services, fire, ambulance and police, are reached by dialing 999 from any phone.

For other serious problems, the American Embassy is at 24 Grosvenor Square, W1 (Bond Street tube station), tel. 499-9000. The Canadian High Commission is in Trafalgar Square, tel. 629-9492; and the Australian High Commission is in The Strand, WC2, tel. 438-8000.

Telephones

The dial tone is a whirring sound. Don't put money in when you hear this; dial, and then (with luck—phone service is erratic) you'll hear the other party pick up the receiver and after one second there'll be an urgent bleeping. Now put in the coin. During your call further urgent bleeps mean that you'll be cut off in about ten seconds unless you insert more money. Money can be put in only while the bleeps are sounding.

You can dial direct to anywhere in the States (dial 0101 and then the American codes). A minute's call will cost only a few dollars, even to the West Coast. From a private phone this is simple, and the cost will be added to the quarterly bill. With public phones there are complications, but the Post Office Telecommunications Office in Trafalgar Square is specially equipped for international calls to be paid for on the spot. Remember, there are different operators for different kinds of calls or information. Also, within England, the area codes do not all have the same number of digits.

Because of vandals and inefficient repairing, many public phones in London don't work. To reduce frustration, try to find a place where there's a row of phones.

Organized Walking Tours

Organized walks around dozens of London districts are available throughout the year and cost very little. The oldest and most reliable organization in this field is called London Walks. Publicity information can be found in the main tourist bureaus. London Walks can also be contacted at 139 Conway Road, Southgate, London N14 7BH, tel. 882-2763. The staff will send information to you in the States (it's appreciated if an international reply coupon is enclosed with your inquiry). Its guides are all enthusiasts operating in their leisure time, and include teachers, bankers and actors. (I can't properly say more about the standard of the guides, because sometimes I'm one of them!)

Glossary

American	British
Subway	Tube, underground ("Subway" in Britain means a tunnel for pedestrians under a main road.)
Excuse me	Sorry ("Excuse me" in Britain means "Please let me through.")
Pants	Trousers ("Pants" in Britain usually means "underclothes.")
Check (in restaurant)	Bill
Restroom, washroom, bathroom	If in public ask for "the ladies" or "the gents" ("Is there a ladies near here?"). In a private house, ask for "the bathroom" or "the loo." "Restroom" will probably not be understood.
Line (of people)	Queue
Two-lane (in same direction)	Dual carriageway
Gasoline	Petrol
Trunk (of an automobile)	Boot
Windshield	Windscreen
Highway	Motorway (marked by signs)
Call collect	Reverse the charges
Busy signal (on telephone)	Engaged tone
Drugstore	Chemist (A dispensing chemist fills prescriptions.)
Sidewalk	Pavement

American	British
Traffic circle	Roundabout
Do you have . . . ?	Have you got . . . ?
Gotten	Got
Truck	Lorry
One-way ticket	Single ticket ("Birmingham, single, please.")
Round-trip ticket	Return ticket (Going to and from on the same day, which is often much cheaper, is called a "cheap day return.")
Here or to go?	Eat here or take away?
First floor	Ground floor ("First floor" in Britain means the second story, "second floor" means the third story, and so on.)
Elevator	Lift
Apartment	Flat
Coffee with cream	White coffee
Dessert	Sweet, pudding
Legal holiday	Bank holiday
Two weeks	Fortnight (14 nights)

Slang	Equivalent
Quid, nicker	Pound (money; written "Two quid," "Three nicker")
Five "p," ten "p," etc.	Five pence, ten pence, etc.
Grotty	Dirty, unattractive
Custom (as in "Thank you for your custom.")	Patronage
Fag	Cigarette
Cheers	Thanks, good-bye
Ta (pronounced "tah")	Thanks

Slang	Equivalent
Mate	Friend
Bird	Girl, woman (a mildly sexist term)
Bloody	An all-purpose swear word; mild but not for polite company.
Stroppy	Indignant, making trouble
All at sea	In difficulties, confused

Tea will come with milk, unless you ask clearly for lemon tea. The word *street* is almost never dropped from the title of a British road; if you ask for Oxford when you are in central London, you'll probably be directed to the city of Oxford, not Oxford Street.

A few final pieces of advice. When you find places that you like, go back to them several times if possible. Repetition helps memory; that way you'll get a photograph in your mind, better than one on film. For finding your way around the areas of London not covered here, I recommend buying the inexpensive book of maps called *A to Z* (*Z* is pronounced "zed" in Britain), which is on sale at many newsstands. Its index is excellent, and often vital for Londoners themselves. It covers all of London—in sections. When meeting British people, remember that occupation more than money determines someone's social class in Britain, so it is polite not to ask directly what job a person does. Don't be put off by the rather reserved British manner. Many British people have come to appreciate American openness and friendliness, and a slight smile or gleam in the eye of a British person can mean "I like you very much."

Walk

1

The London Dickens Knew: Adelphi and Covent Garden

When England emerged from the Middle Ages, there were two cities on the north bank of the lower Thames: the City of London and the City of Westminster. They stood within a couple of miles of each other. The City of London, to the east, was the older, built over the site of Roman Londinium. The Romans themselves hadn't originally intended London to be their capital in Britain; that was to be Camulodunum (now Colchester), more than forty miles away to the northeast. But because they hated seafaring, the Romans weren't willing to sail directly from the Continent to Camulodunum; instead, they landed on the Channel coast and marched toward it, crossing the Thames by bridge at the point where it ceased to be tidal. At the northern end of that bridge traders settled to exploit the traffic, and there Londinium grew up. By A.D. 100 the new settlement had overtaken Camulodunum and become the chief town of Britain.

Roman troops left Britain soon after A.D. 400 to defend richer parts of their crumbling empire. Many centuries later, the Roman walls of London were patched and raised to protect the medieval city. Inside the walls traders and financiers were able to negotiate with monarchs from a position of strength; kings of England normally ruled from Westminster, and thought twice about entering the City of London. As late as the nineteenth century the unpopular King George IV dared not go in for fear of physical attack.

When Londoners say "the City" they still mean the traditional City of London on, or very close to, its Roman site. The City keeps its own Lord Mayor, local government and police; it is also still the headquarters of private finance. Government, too, has stayed in its old place, at Westminster, and goes on dealing cautiously with the financiers down the river. So the tradition of two cities is still alive.

On a later walk (#2) we shall be going inside the western boundary of the City of London. But this walk will be in Westminster, starting on the Embankment,

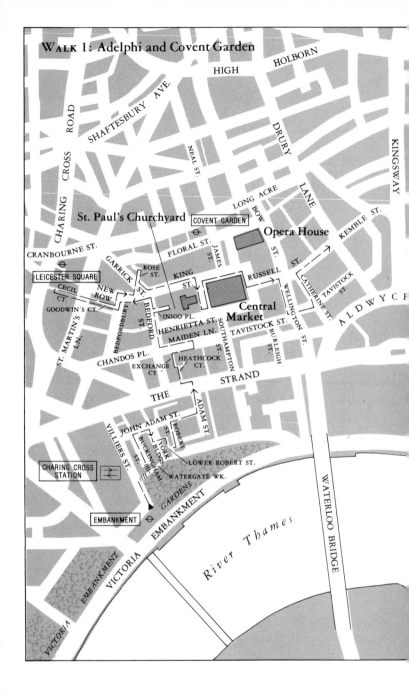

WALK 1: Adelphi and Covent Garden

a piece of land reclaimed from the river in the 1860s. Both parts of our route, the Adelphi and Covent Garden, were well known to Dickens. His father worked nearby as a government clerk, and Dickens himself played here as a child. When his father was imprisoned for debt in 1824, Dickens was put to work in a neighboring factory—at the age of twelve.

In the Adelphi district, most of the streets were laid out in the seventeenth and eighteenth centuries. Several of the original houses survive. The Adelphi itself, as we shall see, was an elegant—and desperate—piece of speculative building by the Adam brothers. (*Adelphi* is Greek for "brothers," and punned on the architects' name.) It was begun in 1768. Today its dignified streets are quiet, and on weekends you'll have the place largely to yourself. But in Dickens's day the area was crowded; riverboats put in at the Adelphi, and their passengers were plundered along the waterfront by a gang of child thieves.

North of the Adelphi is a main road, The Strand. Its name originally meant "the shore"—the river once ran that close. After crossing The Strand, you will reach Covent Garden by a set of dark alleys. Quite safe these days, in the nineteenth century these alleys were a refuge for criminals; they still have the Victorian gaslights that were installed to prevent dark deeds. In Covent Garden itself, dozens of gaslights—some of delicate design, others set on massive iron brackets—are still working. In the Middle Ages the place was a convent garden but after Henry VIII confiscated the property of the Catholic religious orders in the 1530s, the land passed to the Earls (later Dukes) of Bedford. They owned it until 1914, when the 11th Duke sold the entire estate and used much of the proceeds to make what seemed to be a far safer investment—in Russian government bonds. These, of course, collapsed during the revolution three years later.

Much earlier, in the 1630s, the 4th Earl of Bedford had hired the court architect, Inigo Jones, to turn Covent Garden into a grand suburb with Italianate buildings. Although Jones's work in the area has now entirely disappeared, its influence remains, especially in the stylish Central Market buildings constructed in 1830 for the sale of fruit and vegetables. This market trade, already centuries old, was to remain here until 1974, when it was transferred to a site south of the Thames. Now that the fruit and vegetable trucks have gone, Covent Garden is delightfully free of traffic, like a stillness at the center of the whirlpool of London.

Londonwalks

In the evenings, Covent Garden is a middle-class playground—for the hip, the radical and the genteel. A few yards from the Royal Opera House, loud rock music rises from the cellars and from behind the shutters of former vegetable stores. In the daytime, numerous small and unusual shops are run by proud specialists. And for centuries Covent Garden has been the most important place in Britain for authors and publishers to socialize and do business. In the pubs, editors swap horror stories of unreliable authors and authors tell of royalties never seen. Dickens edited a magazine in Covent Garden towards the end of his life, and ate at the best restaurant here. (It still survives, as we shall see.) Many years earlier, in the 1820s, he had wandered in the area as an impoverished child, staring hungrily at the pineapples in the market.

Embankment tube station has two exits; take the one on the left as you come from the ticket barrier, and walk along the right-hand side of the road which runs straight towards you—Villiers Street. The people selling flowers and newspapers here live on the small river of commuters and pleasure-seekers running from the tube to the great railway terminal of Charing Cross at the other end of Villiers Street and to theater-land, one-quarter of a mile beyond.

As you walk away from the tube, with the grim railway bridge on your left, you'll see a pleasant park on your right that is a traditional refuge for a few derelicts. In his book *Down and Out in Paris and London*, George Orwell describes sleeping here himself in the 1930s while living as a vagrant and exploring poverty from the inside. Judging by their accents, the derelicts gathered here nowadays are mostly from northeastern England, Scotland and Ireland. I haven't heard many accents from London or the Midlands, which are more prosperous areas, or from Wales, which is poor but with a strong temperance tradition.

Walk 50 yards along Villiers Street; where the park ends, on the right, is a tiny and eccentric old building, standing alone—one room, a basement and a tall chimney. It is still in use, as the office of an employ-

ment agency that recruits secretaries from the crowds of commuters walking past. In a moment, when you go down the steps right next to this building, look back and you will see that it leans strongly to the north.

The little building happens to mark the line of the old Thames waterfront, before the Embankment was made. The park (called Victoria Embankment Gardens) and the tube station stand where there was once river, or river-mud. The massive building on the left of Villiers Street is Charing Cross Station, constructed partly over the new Embankment in the mid-1860s. It stands over the site of the decrepit shoe-blacking factory where Dickens worked as a child.

He later wrote about the factory and his dreary work in it: "It was a crazy tumbledown old house, abutting of course on the river, and literally overrun with rats. . . . My work was to cover the pots of paste blacking first with a piece of oil paper, and then with a piece of blue paper, to tie them round with string, and then to clip the paper close to them making it neat all round." Dickens's point about rats is probably not an exaggeration. The rat had a great time in nineteenth-century London. One music hall of the period was praised because ladies could sit in it *without* being overrun by rats.

Go down the steps beside the little crooked building into the passageway called Watergate Walk. This was the waterfront of the Thames until the 1860s. You'll see the great stone water gate about 50 yards from the steps, on the right. But first, notice the dingy door on the left, just a few yards beyond the foot of the steps. Behind it is one of London's most pleasant wine bars, Gordon's. There is no sign on the door; this isn't a place many people would find by accident; it thrives on word-of-mouth recommendation. In the days when English wine shops advertised with a small bush hung from a pole, there was a proverb "good wine needs no bush." Gordon's is one of the few places still prepared to trust in that principle. Its wine is reasonably priced, its food outstandingly good value. (Hours are from 11:00–3:00 and 5:30–9:00.)

If you enter, watch out for the steep steps descending into the bar, which is a converted cellar. If you go in the evening, to be sure of a table it's a good idea to arrive at the 5:30 opening time; the place fills very quickly. Your fellow customers will include civil servants from the ministries in Whitehall. Later in the evening there will be people on the way to the theater. Gordon's is a good place to hear the accents of the middle-class and upper-class people who have attended top English private schools. The male speech, often delivered in a throaty drawl, is strong on grand, perhaps condescending, agreement ("Yah," "Absolutely."). Female speech is nasal in tone and more effusive ("My dear, the play was *sim*-ply marvellous. I can't *tell* you how marvellous it was. Too, *too,* funny.") Speech is perhaps the clearest badge of social class in England—much more so than dress, and possibly clearer even than money. In public, upper-class speech tends to be muted, for fear of attracting attention or even satire. But in Gordon's, away from the hoi polloi (who won't pass through the uninviting door), voices can safely be raised a little.

In winter there is an open fire by the bar, and a thick curtain drawn behind the door to prevent drafts. Away from the bar are candlelit tables, the scenes of much amorous anticipation. Sherry is served from wooden casks ("from the wood"), and wine is sold by the bottle or glass. As in pubs, there is no pressure to buy food, but for the price of about three drinks you can get a salad with a selection of superb English cheeses. The choice of food and wine in England again reflects social standing. Social climbers usually prefer French wine (especially champagne) and French cheeses (especially Camembert and Brie). But for those who Really Know, the favorites are Hock (German white wine) and English cheeses. Among the best of these at Gordon's are the Stilton and Red Windsor.

After leaving Gordon's, go a few yards farther along the path to the York Watergate. This hefty triple structure in yellow stone was built in the mid-1620s. It led to a private quay, which stood out over the Thames mud, allowing favored people to land without getting dirty. The water gate was built for one of the most colorful and disastrous figures of the early seventeenth century, George Villiers, Duke of Buckingham. Buckingham's grand residence, York House, stood where

Gordon's now stands, and his gardens stretched across the site of the present Buckingham Street.

Born in 1592, George Villiers was to become the favorite, first of King James I and then of James's son, Charles I. Although not of aristocratic family, he shot up the court hierarchy (due to his good looks, popular belief had it) and was promoted within eight years to viscount, earl, marquis and finally duke. King James clumsily defended his support of Buckingham thus: "You may be sure that I love the Earl of Buckingham more than anyone else . . . Christ had his John, and I have my George." By 1625, when James died and was succeeded by Charles, Buckingham had become virtually ruler of England.

Buckingham used his power with an appalling lack of skill. In 1623 he and Charles had gone to Spain to arrange a marriage between Charles and the Spanish princess. The attempt failed, and Buckingham insulted the Spanish court. Later he also insulted the court of France by making amorous advances in public to their queen. In a war with France shortly thereafter, Buckingham led a naval expedition against French forces at La Rochelle; he was defeated and lost most of his men. Parliament bitterly objected to Buckingham's power and tried to impeach him. Enough anonymous poems were written against him to fill a small book. Buckingham took part in a ballet here at York House; the following is a poem contrasting the stern English warriors of old with this dancing courtier who attempted to fight the French.

> Rejoyce, brave English gallants,
>   whose ancestors won France,
> Our Duke of Buckingham is gone
>   to fight and not to dance.
> Believe it; for our ladies
>   his absence greatly mourn;
> And swear they'll have no babies
>   until he doth return.

One unofficial notice about Buckingham was nailed up in the City of London: "Who rules the kingdom? The King. Who rules the King? The Duke. Who rules the Duke? The Devil. Let the Duke look to it." This was slang, meaning "He'd better watch out." Buckingham did not "look to it" with enough care. In 1628, while preparing another foreign military adventure, he was stabbed in the chest by an aggrieved ex–naval officer. He called out "Villain," staggered and died. King Charles blamed Parliament for encouraging Buckingham's assassin. Their quarrel helped lead eventually to the Civil Wars of the 1640s and to Charles's own violent death on the scaffold at Whitehall.

Buckingham's water gate reflects his career. He lived on this site only because he had unscrupulously evicted the previous occupant of York House, the philosopher and politician Francis Bacon. Above the two outer bays of the gate, visible from Watergate Walk, are stones carved in the shape of anchors. These were meant to remind people of Buckingham's role as admiral. His coat of arms, over the central arch, has a duke's coronet shown above it to advertise his social success. The inscription in Latin, which runs across all three bays, is Buckingham's pious family motto, *Fidei Coticula Crux* ("The cross is the touchstone of faith"). To see how the gate was meant to look from the river, either go through it, or, if it's locked, go around into the park by way of the entrance which is just the other side of the crooked house. The water gate was designed in an Italian style, which was the one approved by the court at the time. On the river side it has attached columns with artificially roughened bands. This rustication is an Italian device to make architecture look countrified.

York House itself was sold in the early 1670s by Buckingham's son, the 2nd Duke. It was demolished shortly afterwards, and streets were laid out over the site. Of the home of the scandalous Buckingham, only his water gate now remains.

Go up the double set of steps just opposite the water gate into Buckingham Street. The first building on the right (nos. 15–16) is the only modern one in the street. It stands on the site of a house where Dickens lived briefly as a young journalist in 1834 and which he used as part of the setting of *David Copperfield*. Dickens's houses in London, like this one in Buckingham Street, have nearly all been destroyed. The one important house left, in Doughty Street (near Chancery Lane tube station), is kept as a Dickens museum.

The seventeenth- and eighteenth-century houses in Buckingham Street are tall and mostly flat-fronted. The best rooms—those with the tallest windows and highest ceilings—are on the second story.* Look across the street at no. 11. The grand second-story rooms were designed to be as different as possible from the servants' quarters. Servants lived under the roof, with small windows—and the noise of the pigeons. The master and his family avoided living on the top floor because that was the most dangerous place in the event of a fire.

This street was begun less than ten years after the Great Fire of 1666, in which most of the City of London was destroyed. For the builders of Buckingham Street fire prevention was definitely a consideration—even so, several of the houses did eventually burn down (nos. 13 and 14 in 1684 and no. 19 in 1794).

Outside no. 18 are traces of elegant living—and of fire precautions—from the 1700s: hollow cones of iron, set on a frame on each side of the door. The cones, called "link extinguishers," were used at night to put out torches (links). Until the coming of gas lighting, in the early nineteenth century, link boys were hired to run, torches blazing, in front of a carriage to guide it past potholes and obstacles. Crime flourished in the dark streets; the link boys, in reality often men, were also meant to serve as a defense against robbery. Once the passengers had alighted, the torches—commonly made with tar or candle wax—were extinguished by being thrust into the iron cones. (The link boys would have put out their torches anyway for the sake of economy, and if they did so by trampling them on the ground a fire might break out in the litter in the street.) Link extinguishers were also a sign that you were expecting grand guests, the sort who could afford a carriage and link boys. Many of the surviving eighteenth- and early-nineteenth-century houses in London were originally artisans' dwellings and have been revamped in recent years. But link extinguishers show that a house was already a grand residence more than 150 years ago.

Notice the light—the small window directly above the door—at no. 18; it is divided by strips of metal in the shape of a fan. Traditionally, different houses on

*British usage for referring to floors of buildings is employed throughout. See p. 16.

a street had different lights, perhaps for purposes of identification before house numbers came into use. No. 13, across the street, has a different style of fan-light; no. 17's light is in a diamond pattern.

From 1697, no. 13 was the home of Dr. William Coward, a well-known religious heretic. Coward argued that the soul was never separated from the body, and that soul and body would rise together at the resurrection. Today it might be difficult to find Christians sure that this doctrine *is* heretical, let alone why it is. But in Coward's day interest in Protestant theology was intense. In 1704 the House of Commons discussed his writings, and ordered them to be burned by the common hangman, a practice both humiliating and frightening to the writer. Of course it also increased public interest in Coward's books.

Samuel Pepys lived for nine years, starting in 1679, at no. 12 Buckingham Street, and the house has changed little since his day. In England, because of his delightful diary, Pepys's name is probably the best known of any English writer between the times of Shakespeare and Dickens. The main diary runs from 1660 to 1669, when Pepys was in his twenties and thirties, and before he lived in Buckingham Street. It shows him to have been a man of unusual self-awareness. Like Dickens, Pepys had great energy both for work and women. His diary gives lively backstairs details about Charles II's court and about Pepys's own home.

As a boy, Pepys had seen the execution of Charles I and had definitely approved. In the 1660s, with the dead king's son, Charles II, on the throne, he was frightened that someone would remember this. Nevertheless, he quietly kept some republican sympathies and was upset by the punishment of Charles I's old enemies: "This afternoon . . . I saw the limbs of some of our new traitors set upon Aldersgate in the City of London, which was a sad sight to see; and a bloody week this and the last have been, there being ten hanged, drawn and quartered."

Pepys got his first post in Charles II's civil service through the influence of a relative. He admitted to himself that he had depended on nepotism, and needed to work hard to survive: "Chance without merit brought me in, and diligence only keeps me so, and will [do], living as I do among so many lazy people that the diligent man becomes necessary, that they cannot do anything without him." But he explained to himself why pleasure, too, was needed: "The truth is, I do indulge myself a little more in pleasure, knowing that this is the proper age of my life to do it [he was in his early thirties at the time]; and, out of my observation that most men that do thrive in the world do forget to take pleasure during the time they are getting their estate, but reserve that till they have got one, and then it is too late for them to enjoy it."

Pepys thought the King had a bit too much pleasure with the royal mistresses: "The King do spend most of his time in feeling and kissing them naked . . . this lechery will never leave him." But Pepys took similar pleasures. When he fell in love with his maid, Deb Willett, his wife found out and there were great quarrels. Once Mrs. Pepys got so angry that "she came to my side of the bed and drew my curtain open, and with the tongs, red hot at the ends, made as if she did design to pinch me with them." But he shrewdly noticed that this quarrel about Deb improved his marital relations in one way: "I have lain with my *moher* ["wife" in Spanish] as a husband more times since this falling-out than in, I believe, twelve months before—and with more pleasure to her than, I think, in all the time of our marriage before."

For much of his life Pepys was the most important administrator of the British navy. He became rich, partly by using—or abusing—his power to award contracts. But he describes one bribe which he did not want: some expensive fish, sent to persuade him to accept overpriced tar from a Mr. Bowyer. Pepys decided to say no to Mr. Bowyer, though he received "last night, as a bribe, a barrel of sturgeon, which, it may be, I shall send back, for I will not have the King abused so abominably in the price of what we buy . . ."

In May 1679, during an anti-Catholic panic, Pepys was accused of leaking information about the navy to the government of Catholic France and of plotting against Protestantism. He was locked up for a time in the Tower of London, but the prosecution case collapsed. Pepys was released and given even more pow-er over naval affairs. It was at about this time that he first came to live in Buckingham Street. From no. 12 he ran the navy. In 1688 he moved just down the street to a grander house, which has not survived but which stood on the site of the present no. 14.

That same year, after a reign of only three years, Charles II's Catholic brother James II was driven out of England by a Protestant invasion. This was bad news for Pepys, who had been given the job of organizing James's navy to keep the invaders out. Since Pepys was suspected of remaining secretly loyal to the exiled James, he was imprisoned in 1689, under the new King, William III. But he was soon released, and al-though he lost his control of the navy, he seems to have ended his life a popular man. Until 1701 (two years before his death) he remained owner of the house that stood down by the water gate.

At the top of Buckingham Street turn right into John Adam Street and walk to the next corner on the right (where John Adam Street joins York Buildings). You are now on the edge of the Adelphi, the streets created by Robert, James and William Adam between 1768 and 1774. Their designs were inspired by fine Italian houses. Look ahead of you, to the very end of John Adam Street. The house facing down the street was decorated by the brothers with especially bold lines; it was meant to be impressive at a distance to people coming up John Adam Street, as you're doing now. From here you can see that it has four tall pilasters in its façade—flat-fronted columns built into the brick. Soon after they were finished, the Adelphi buildings were berated by a writer who said they were "ware-houses, laced down the seams," and looked like a sol-dier's tart dressed in a regimental coat. This was harsh criticism, but seeing the house from a distance helps to explain it.

When the brothers began to build here, the land sloped very steeply down to the Thames. So Robert Adam, the chief architect, lessened the gradient by building great rows of arches to support his streets as they approached the river. These arches were extreme-ly expensive, and in 1773, before the Adelphi was fin-ished, the Adams' funds ran out. A vast lottery was held to raise money to complete the project; over

4,300 tickets were issued at £50 each. The prizes were to be the houses, warehouses, shops and storage vaults of the Adelphi. Fifty pounds was a large sum at that time; eighty years later common soldiers were earning less than £20 a year. But gambling was highly popular with the middle- and upper-classes in eighteenth-century England, and many of the tickets were no doubt bought by syndicates. Some of the winners quickly sold their prizes, and thus could divide their winnings.

Dickens wrote in *David Copperfield*: "I was fond of wandering about the Adelphi, because it was a myste-

Brass knocker, door of Royal Society of the Arts

rious place with those dark arches." The centerpiece of the Adams' scheme, Adelphi Terrace, was demolished in the 1930s and most of the arches are gone. But you can still see one: turn into the street called York Buildings and 15 yards along go left into Lower Robert Street, which dives underground; it may look grim but it is quite safe. There's no proper sidewalk, so watch out for the cars which swoop up and down here. Just after you go underground, and before turning to the right, you'll pass under one of the original dark arches.

Go under the arch, turn right and head for the daylight about 100 yards ahead. Fifteen yards before you come out into light, look through the small iron gate on the right. The dark, sordid yard behind preserves the spirit of the Dickensian underworld. The wall on the right of the yard belongs to the basement of a lofty, fashionable Adam house. You will see its decorated pilasters in a few minutes when you reach the street above. But here below were the social depths.

It was from nooks like this, underneath the Adelphi, that the child thieves operated in the early 1840s. The children specialized in stealing expensive silk handkerchiefs from gentlemen's coattail pockets. One thief, who was interviewed as an adult in the early 1860s, told a story very much like that of Dickens's *Oliver Twist*. He had run away to London at the age of nine and gone to live in a slum at Field Lane—an evil street, now demolished, west of St. Paul's Cathedral. Later he joined the child thieves here at the Adelphi, sleeping with them in a derelict van under the arches. Their thief-master was named not Fagin but Larry, and he threatened those children who did not bring him their stolen handkerchiefs with disclosure to the police. Only those who obeyed him were allowed to sleep in the van.

Dickens's *Oliver Twist* was realistic about the way many stray children were forced to live in early-nineteenth-century England. Easy to frighten and control, these urchins were useful to thief-masters: their touch for picking pockets was more delicate than most adults'; police were hesitant to arrest small children; and, even if caught and convicted, children were less likely than adults to be transported to Australia.

Victorian thieves' retreat,
Lower Robert Street

On leaving the underground road, you'll come out into York Place, once the waterfront and now hemmed in with gardens. Go up the steps that begin a few feet away to your left. At the top is a large office block of the 1930s. It is out of scale with the Adam streets around it, and its masses of glass and concrete clash with the delicate decoration of the eighteenth-century buildings. Look at the vast concrete statues at the corners of the office block, and then at the elaborate pilasters of the Adam house opposite (nos. 2–3 Robert Street). The architects of the office block—Collcutt and Hamp—made way for their scheme by knocking down the Adelphi Terrace, which was the heart of the eighteenth-century Adelphi.

Turn your back to the offices, and look out over the low wall towards the river. Below you is a pleasant view of the park on the Thames Embankment. In the 1860s, the novelist Thomas Hardy trained as an architect here in Adelphi Terrace and watched the Embankment being built. He later used his knowledge of architecture to create the character of George Somerset, the architect-hero of *A Laodicean* (one of the very few of Hardy's novels that does not end in tragedy).

Through the trees to the left, at the river's edge, you can see the top of Cleopatra's Needle, the ancient Egyptian obelisk which was set up on the Embankment in 1878. Some mementos of the 1870s were buried beneath it, including Bradshaw's Railway Timetable and portraits of Lillie Langtry, the mistress of the heir to the throne. More on her in a little while.

Walk the 100 yards or so of Robert Street, with its Adam houses on the left and Collcutt and Hamp on the right. When you reach the corner with John Adam Street you will see, slightly to the right, perhaps the prettiest section of the whole Adelphi scheme: the home of the Royal Society of Arts. It would make a lovely advertisement for Britain as many of the British would like it to appear.

The doorway of the building, which dates from 1774, is decorated with string-molding, almost a trademark of Robert Adam's work. Above the doorway is a large window, fan-shaped at the top in a Venetian style. Miniature Ionic Greek columns on each side of

the window help to divide the façade. And to prevent a feeling of heaviness in the pediment (the shallow triangle under the roof), Adam included a small, circular window to break up the expanse of brickwork.

The Royal Society of Arts was founded in 1754 to encourage inventors. It still does. A gold medal was recently awarded here to an engineer, Eric Donald, who had designed an aircraft bolt to give early warning of metal fatigue. The bolt is hollow and filled with dye; if it cracks it "bleeds" visibly onto the surface of the plane. The presentation of the medal here brought important early publicity for the invention. So Robert Adam's elegant building is still doing its job.

Pass the front of the building, and go a few yards, to the corner of Adam Street. No. 7 Adam Street is the building you noticed a while ago from a distance. From here you can see that the pilasters and door frame have an intricate set of moldings. Adam decoration like this, especially string-moldings around fireplaces and doors, later became highly fashionable; connoisseurs of late-eighteenth-century buildings still look eagerly for it. But, at the time, many architects found the style effeminate and silly. One of them, Sir William Chambers, who preferred a simpler and more massive style of building, is said to have persuaded King George III not to give Robert Adam a knighthood. Shortly after the building of the Adelphi, Chambers put up one of his own portly constructions close by, no doubt expecting people to see its superiority. This was Somerset House, a set of government buildings, which still stands (with additions) about 300 yards east of the Adelphi. It was in Somerset House that Dickens's imprudent father worked as a clerk in the Admiralty.

No. 8 Adam Street, with its fine doorcase, was owned from 1788 to 1792 by Richard Arkwright, one of the pioneers of the Industrial Revolution. Arkwright's great invention was the spinning frame, a machine that used the power of water or steam to convert raw cotton into thread. He made a fortune by exploiting this invention in factories in the north of England. His competitors copied it, and Arkwright probably took this expensive town house for its nearness to the London courts, where he spent much time defending his legal rights as inventor.

About 40 yards to the north Adam Street ends at The Strand—a traffic-ridden highway between Westminster and the City. Cross The Strand at the pedestrian crossing a few yards to the left. (A child recently described pedestrian crossings rather well: "They're places where cars aren't allowed to knock you down.") When you are across the street, look right, toward the City, at the two fine churches that stand in the middle of the road, one behind the other, like islands in the river of steel. The nearer one is St. Mary's-le-Strand (Dickens's parents were married here in 1809). The French *le* in the name is a trace of the last conquest of England; William of Normandy and his associates, who captured England in 1066, spoke French, and French remained the everyday language of the court for over three centuries. The church farther away is St. Clement Danes, badly bombed in the last war but now restored to the seventeenth-century design of Christopher Wren. This is the church mentioned in the traditional nursery rhyme about London bells:

> "Oranges and lemons," say the bells of St.
>   Clement's,
> "You owe me five farthings," say the bells of
>   St. Martin's,
> "When will you pay me?" say the bells of Old
>   Bailey,
> "When I am rich," say the bells of Shoreditch.

About a yard from the end of the pedestrian crossing, in the direction of the two churches there's an entrance to a dark alley, Heathcock Court. (It isn't clearly marked; look underneath the sign for Barclays Bank, no. 415 The Strand.) Walking up the alley, you will come to your first Covent Garden gaslight. There are two lamps here. In the daytime the timing mechanism of the first ticks away unnoticed, just a few yards from the modern noise of The Strand. At night in this little-used passage, you'll see that both lamps are badly needed.

Gas lighting became common in London around 1820 and was only slowly squeezed out by electric lighting at the end of the century. In 1878 gas stocks crashed on the London exchange; people thought that the age of electricity had already arrived. But the shares soon made a comeback. For one thing, poor people were reluctant to part with their gaslights because they gave out a slight heat. Also, by the end of the nineteenth century, the newest types of gaslight were so bright that, for street lighting, there wasn't much difference between them and electricity. Perhaps the main reason for their eventual disuse was the cost of the labor needed to maintain them.

Victorian writers themselves, as well as modern filmmakers, have used gas lighting as a romantic setting. This sentimental song is about a Victorian flower-seller:

> Underneath the gaslight's glitter
> Stands a little, fragile girl,
> Heedless of the night winds bitter
> As they round about her whirl;
>
> While the hundreds pass unheeding
> In the evening's waning hours,
> Still she cries, with tearful pleading,
> "Won't you buy my pretty flowers?"

Moving stuff! Victorian writers loved children—especially when they were dying.

The reason for installing gaslights in the first place was not at all sentimental. In 1823 the parish of Hampstead bought gaslights for its own streets because they were "the most efficient aid to the police in the repression and detection of offenders in the streets and highways." And in these grim passages north of The Strand it is easy to see why.

Turn right at the second gaslight, just 30 yards from The Strand, and follow Heathcock Court around to its blind corner on the left, passing through the modern gate. This splendidly evil spot is surrounded by high and dark nineteenth-century walls, with just a small patch of sky visible far above. There always seems to be a pigeon here, which goes scrambling out of the brickwork when disturbed, leaving the walls echoing to the clatter of its wings. On the left is the unused iron bracket of a gas lamp, which was only replaced by a dismal electric light in 1979. The old wall on the right has its windows barred with iron, against nineteenth-century climbers. The set of bars on the wall directly facing you, about twelve feet from the ground, is carefully maintained. The little window behind the bars, part of the Adelphi Theatre, belongs to a retiring room kept for royalty. Also in this dark corner is a long-forgotten box-office window. The theater wall here survives from Dickens's day. Several works of his were dramatized and performed at the Adelphi, including (in the 1840s) *A Christmas Carol.*

Coming out of this dark corner, you will see that the support of the modern fire escape on the left boasts another device to deter climbers—a set of curved spikes, some pointing up and some down. Turn to the right and go straight down the path, keeping on your left the gaslight you saw earlier. Within 30 yards, the path makes a T junction with another alley, Exchange Court. Turn right, and 50 yards up the alley you will see Maiden Lane. On the way there, look over the wall on the left or through the grille in its gate at the backs of tall, bleak nineteenth-century slums.

When the alley emerges into Maiden Lane, turn right. A few yards along on the right, where the road widens slightly, are the rear doors of the Adelphi Theatre. (Its entrance is on The Strand.) Above the first door is a crude molding of the royal coat of arms. This "royal entrance" is used as a stage door, and in 1897 it was the scene of a famous murder. William Terriss, a leading actor of the period, was entering the theater one night by the stage door when he was stabbed to death. The killer, a minor actor, seems to have believed insanely that, with Terriss dead, he himself could become famous in Terriss's place. He was arrested, raving, a few yards away in Maiden Lane, and only his madness saved him from the scaffold. The ghost of William Terriss features in some of the more interesting stories of Covent Garden hauntings. Many ghost stories from this area originate with actors, and you can't help wondering how many of them have merely been testing their acting skills by trying to convince people of spooky nonsense. But in 1955 two rather more believable people, workers at Covent Garden tube station, were separately frightened by the figure of a man with old-fashioned clothes and pale gloves. One of them said he had tried to question the man, who then vanished in front of his eyes. The other, when shown a photo of Terriss, is said to have claimed immediately that this was the person he had seen.

A few yards farther down Maiden Lane, on the other side, is no. 35, Rule's restaurant. Inside, the dining rooms are still furnished in their Victorian style. Paintings and prints from the nineteenth century cover most of the walls; and there is a gleam of dark wood from the sideboards and chairs. Dickens used to visit Rule's in the last years of his life. Tradition has it that his favorite table was in an alcove at the rear of the second story. The alcove is out of the sight of most of the diners, so this would certainly have been a good place for the famous author to find some privacy.

In the 1870s the restaurant was a favorite of the

Dickensian restaurant, Maiden Lane

Prince of Wales, later to become King Edward VII. His special table was in the alcove at the front of the second story, by the window at the far right (looking from the street). Edward used to come here with his mistress, Lillie Langtry. He was already married and had children (one of whom, incidentally, was later to be suspected of being Jack the Ripper, the murderer of 1888; see pages 115–16), so Edward, understandably, was very anxious for privacy when dining here à deux with Lillie. His alcove was curtained off, and a special doorway was built that enabled him to enter the alcove without being seen by other diners. The curtain has been removed, but the doorway is still there. Lillie Langtry's portrait now hangs in the alcove.

Rule's still has a fairly well-heeled clientele. Cabinet ministers sometimes dine here. Princess Margaret and Prince Charles ate here quite recently. The prices aren't extravagant, but take note that credit cards are not accepted. As well as more exotic dishes, Rule's serves roast beef and Yorkshire pudding, which makes it unusual among good London restaurants. Middle- and upper-class people in England like to eat un-English food when they dine out; beef and Yorkshire pudding are things they can always get at home. The result for foreign visitors is that these traditional English dishes are often unobtainable.

If you eat at Rule's, the staff will gladly show you the two famous alcoves. And from the street have a look at the worn brass plate by the door on the right that advertises the restaurant. Replacing it with a new one would be unthinkable; an old plate shows that you have been trading successfully for many years, and is also very chic, particularly if it's been polished so much that it's almost unreadable.

Go back down Maiden Lane, passing the back of the Adelphi Theatre again, until you come to the corner on the right with Bedford Street. At this corner, nos. 39–40 Bedford Street, are the offices of a very British magazine, *The Lady*. Founded in Covent Garden in 1885 as *The Lady, A Journal for Gentlewomen*, it has been on its present site since 1891. A thoughtful and pleasant magazine, *The Lady* still contains interesting traces of aristocratic British society. Ladies who advertise for servants in the magazine expect their titles to be helpful. One recent advertisement read:

> TITLED LADY requires full- or part-time living-in nurse
> companion.

There are also advertisements for nannies and governesses. *The Lady* has many articles on travel—a tradition that perhaps dates back to the days of the British Empire. Many of its readers must have been the wives and daughters of colonial administrators and businessmen, and even back in England these ladies would have kept an affectionate interest in remote and sunny lands. Today *The Lady*'s readership is largely middle class, and definitely unrebellious; but the magazine is not a cozy and uncritical journal for homemakers. Over the years it has quietly supported the rights of professional women, and now, as the magazine becomes more modern, it is losing most of its aristocratic flavor. When it expresses strong criticism, the tone is acidic rather than strident—exactly the style of genteelly educated English women. (It calls to mind the words of the discreet but formidable Florence Nightingale who in the 1850s criticized the mountainous, self-indulgent women who were then practicing nursing. "Drunken dames of 14 stone and over must be barred," she wrote. "The provision of bedsteads is not strong enough.") To understand *The Lady* and the genteel women it addresses, you need an eye for wry humor and understatement, ways in which English ladies have traditionally made their point.

Turn right and go up Bedford Street, crossing Henrietta Street on the right, until you come to a small court, also on the right, called Inigo Place. This is the entrance to the churchyard of St. Paul's Covent Garden (not to be confused with St. Paul's Cathedral, a quite separate building about a mile to the east of here). The coat of arms, with lion and scallop shells, above the gates into Inigo Place is that of the Dukes of Bedford, who used to own the district. The churchyard is large and quiet, shut in by the backs of nineteenth-century buildings with tall, slender windows. The buildings form a windbreak, making this a fine place to rest on a sunny day. The churchyard isn't easy to spot from the road, and it is not often discovered by visitors. The locals know it, though, and in summer often come here for a picnic lunch.

In the evening the churchyard is a romantic and little-used spot, with a double line of low gas lamps running to the front of the church. By standing on one of the wooden seats, you can examine a lamp's mechanism. You will see that the pipe that carries the gas comes up through the center of the lamp standard. The lamps are crowned by models of a ducal coronet—homage, again, to the Dukes of Bedford. The lamp farthest to the right, at the front of the church, has its coronet prettily painted.

The church itself is Italian in style, with a shallowly angled roof and two large bells housed in the pediment. It is a late-eighteenth-century replacement of a burned seventeenth-century original. The original was built in the same style and was a vital part of Inigo Jones's grand design for Covent Garden.

Long before the coming of the gas lamps, in 1670 this churchyard is said to have been the scene of a sinister funeral by torchlight. The dead man was Claude Duval, a Frenchman from Normandy and a highwayman, reputed to be a chivalrous robber and ladies' man. Duval was hanged at Tyburn in West London, and respected reference books say that he was buried here at St. Paul's Church with a striking poem inscribed on his gravestone:

Here lies Du Vall: reader, if male thou art,
Look to thy purse; if female, to thy heart.
Much havoc has he made of both: for all
Men he made stand, and women he made fall.
The second conqueror of the Norman race,
Knights to his arms did yield, and ladies to his face.
Old Tyburn's glory, England's illustrious thief,
Du Vall the ladies' joy, Du Vall the ladies' grief.

Glamorous highwaymen breed legends, and—as we'll see in a moment—there may be more to this poem than meets the eye. Within months of Duval's execution, a satire was published anonymously which reported a story of the highwayman's gallantry. One day Duval was robbing a coach that happened to have a young lady in it. She,

to shew she was not afraid, takes a flageolet out of her pocket and plays. Du Vall takes the hint, plays also, and excellently well, upon a flageolet of his own. . . . Sir, says he to the person in the coach, your lady plays excellently, and I doubt not but that she dances as well, will you please to walk out of the coach, and let me have the honour to dance . . . with her upon the heath?

They danced, then Duval showed his courtesy by robbing the couple of only £100, although he knew that they had another £300 in their coach. He called the theft "paying for the music."

The satire hints strongly that Duval was bisexual, saying that in France no one of either sex could resist him, and goes on to "report" the poem in the church here. A close look at the poem shows that it makes—cleverly and discreetly—a similar point about his sexual tastes. "Knights to his arms did yield, and ladies to his face" contains a pun. "All men he made stand, and women he made fall" has a similar double meaning; the word *stand* is often used like this by risqué seventeenth- and eighteenth-century writers. If this interpretation is right, the poem was probably too naughty to have been inscribed in a church. It isn't in St. Paul's Church now, and there seems to be no serious record of anyone's ever having seen it there. I suspect it never was there: the satirist made it up for fun, and has accidentally deceived local historians who haven't looked at his work carefully. (I have found a record of Duval's burial in the register of St. Giles's Church nearby, which helps to bear out this theory.)

Returning from the churchyard to Bedford Street, turn right and walk to the next corner, King Street. Across the road on the other corner of Bedford Street is Moss Bros., pronounced "Moss Bross," a formal-wear shop that is a household name in Britain. The company was founded in the nineteenth century by Moses Moses, a clothing dealer from Maiden Lane. One observer, commenting on all the rented finery at the Royal Coronation in 1953, claimed that "without Moss Bros., Queen Elizabeth's coronation could scarcely have taken place." This was perhaps a slight exaggeration—you can't help suspecting that the British upper class might just have made it to the Coronation without the help of the Bedford Street clothing firm.

The street that runs towards Bedford Street here and helps form the corner where Moss Bros. stands is New Row. Fifty yards along, at no. 12 New Row, is a building that used to be a fruit and vegetable warehouse in the days of Covent Garden market. Today antique scientific instruments are sold here. Arthur Middleton, who owns the business, is a surveyor by training. Many of the instruments he sells were made for navigation in the nineteenth century or earlier—sextants and hand-held naval telescopes.

The shop gleams with brass. The large amounts of brass used in antique instruments helped eventually to make them very scarce. During both world wars, the authorities in German-occupied Europe demanded that old instruments be given up so that the brass could be reused for armaments. Surviving instruments are usually expensive, and only at Christmas does Mr. Middleton stock instruments costing less than £50. His catalog circulates internationally. The antique medical instruments sold here have proved popular with physicians, as conversation pieces or toys. I was shown a device for trepanning—drilling holes in the human skull. Devices like this were used long before anesthetics. I was also shown a jar for keeping leeches, the charming little creatures used by doctors for sucking out human blood. Doctors in England practiced bleeding their patients until the 1920s. The word *leech* came to have two meanings: the little worms themselves, and the doctors who used them. One Victorian dictionary in England said dryly, "*Leech*: a blood-sucking worm; a physician."

Running into New Row on the left here is the street called Bedfordbury. Five yards down the street at no. 25 is Catz, a shop specializing in feline mementos. There are umbrellas, aprons, ornaments, all decorated with pictures of cats. Most of the goods seem to be for human use only. It would be nice to see rather more things—like felt mice, for instance—that cats themselves could enjoy.

A few steps farther down Bedfordbury, between nos. 23 and 24, you'll find an unremarkable entry labeled Goodwin's Court. Few Londoners notice it, so Goodwin's Court is still a superbly preserved and almost secret eighteenth-century street. Go a few steps up the entry from Bedfordbury; along the south side of the court is a row of narrow houses with bow fronts. Parts of these houses date back to the end of the seventeenth century, but bow fronts were not used

until the mid-eighteenth century. Look through some of the windows; the rooms behind them are tiny. The small staircase to the next story begins in the front room because there is no back room or hall.

Walk 20 yards down the court, past the smell of curry from the kitchen of an Indian restaurant, and look back at the house built over the entry to the court. When occasional parties of visitors do penetrate Goodwin's Court, the second-story window of this house often swings open and Mr. Tony Sympson appears. Sympson is a successful actor who has appeared with Julie Andrews in London and on American TV with Danny Kaye and Mia Farrow in *Peter Pan*. He enjoys giving free entertainment to people who have come to admire this little street. From his window he tells them about its history, and before the window swings shut again, he will end with a saucy limerick.

Goodwin's Court owes a lot to Mr. Sympson and his family. When the Sympsons first moved here, around 1930, the court was a slum alley—a survivor of the old Bedfordbury hovels that Dickens mentioned in *Bleak House*. Residents sat shelling peas on their doorsteps. Children ran barefoot across the alley. Late at night one drunken old dame used to relieve herself simply by lifting her skirts over a grating. The court was then condemned and slated for demolition by the local authority; its residents were mostly rehoused. But one of Mr. Sympson's brothers bravely defied the order and restored part of the court so beautifully that the row of seventeenth-century houses was allowed to remain. The two bow fronts nearest you as you enter from Bedfordbury were rebuilt; the rest are from the eighteenth century. This row of old houses is still owned, and beautifully maintained, by the Sympsons, who are rightly proud of what they have saved for London. At night, when the light from the Victorian gas lamps is reflected in the long line of bow windows, this quiet courtyard is perhaps one of the finest places in the city.

Underneath Mr. Sympson's window is a prettily painted metal plaque about nine inches long. It shows a building in the City of London—the Royal Exchange, the headquarters of the company that once owned the sign. This is a fire mark, a badge used from the early 1700s until 1833 to show that a building was protected

Antique scientific instruments,
Covent Garden

by a particular insurance company. At that time the only effective fire brigades were those organized by private insurance firms. The firemen in these brigades would often refuse to use their equipment on a burning building unless it was insured with their company. Since owners could hardly be expected to produce their insurance documents during a fire, the insurance companies insisted that their clients affix metal fire marks outside their buildings. The marks, often made by women, had many attractive designs and made good advertisements. Nowadays a fire mark on a house suggests that it had a prosperous owner 150 years ago or more. The fire marks also proved to be insurance against one's enemies. In the eighteenth century, if you didn't like someone, a fairly common way to express your animosity was to burn the person's house down. But if you saw a fire mark you might think twice. The penalties for arson were severe, and if your enemy was insured anyway, why bother?

Competition between insurance companies sometimes led to wild scenes. If a burning building had a rich owner, or was insured with more than one company, rival brigades were eager to arrive first at the fire, to collect the special reward laid down by law. Horse-drawn fire engines, painted in the companies' liveries, raced each other through the streets. The firemen sometimes brawled and slashed at each other's hoses. Company firemen were not always paid a retainer, but rather were rewarded for each fire attended. One of the attractions of serving in a company brigade was that you got legal protection from the press-gang—the government organization that virtually kidnapped men and forced them to join the navy.

If a company brigade wouldn't help at a fire, the victims had to hope that they might get a little help from the parish fire engine, which was supported with local taxes. These engines could be absurdly inefficient, as Dickens describes:

> We never saw a parish engine at a regular fire but once. It came up in gallant style—three miles and a half an hour at least. . . . Bang went the pumps, the people cheered, the beadle [a parish official] perspired profusely, but it was unfortunately discovered . . . that nobody under-

Goodwin's Court

stood the process by which the engine was filled with water, and that 18 boys and a man had exhausted themselves in pumping 20 minutes without producing the slightest effect!

Leave Goodwin's Court by the far end, where it joins St. Martin's Lane. Across this busy road, a few yards to the left, is another gaslit passage, Cecil Court. On the corner, at 94 St. Martin's Lane, is Freed's, the best-known shop for ballet shoes and costumes in this theatrical district.

In Cecil Court itself most of the shops sell second-hand books, maps and prints. At no. 2, Anglebooks specializes in books on angling and English local history. At no. 4, selling Welsh books and maps, is Griffs. Griffs opened in 1945, when the four Welsh-speaking Griffiths brothers moved here from their home in South Wales. During the war the building had contained an air-raid shelter. Afterwards, it was a difficult job making the shelves needed for the bookshop because wood was being rationed. So, friends of the brothers organized themselves to obtain the wood one pound at a time, that being the limit per person. The basement of the shop became a haven for travelers and exiles from Wales, a place where Welsh people could feel safe in the foreign city of London. Two of the brothers, John and Arthur Griffiths, still run the shop. When I first visited, Mrs. Mary Griffiths asked me, *"Siaradwch chi Gymraeg?"* ("Do you speak Welsh?") Mr. Arthur Griffiths will show you a cupboard in the basement where the best-known Welsh writer of this century, Dylan Thomas, kept the manuscript of his play *Under Milk Wood.* In the basement, too, are books in the Welsh language. Elsewhere in London there are very few signs of Welsh, though it is Britain's second language, with about one million speakers. In large areas of North and West Wales it's the primary language. Welsh is descended from the Celtic language that was spoken in most of Britain before the Romans came. The name London probably originated from this early form of Welsh. Germanic invaders after A.D. 400 brought the language that became English. Welsh then slowly retreated to the far west of Britain, leaving behind many place names. That is why England has several River Avons: *Avon*, spelled *afon*, is the Welsh word for river.

Griffs is on the western edge of Covent Garden. To see the old market and the center of Covent Garden you will need to retrace your route a few hundred yards. I suggest going back up Goodwin's Court. Where it ends, turn left into Bedfordbury and then right, by the shop with the scientific instruments, into New Row. After about 50 yards, New Row ends at the five-road intersection we saw earlier. The second exit here, working clockwise from your left, is narrow, quiet and paved with flagstones—Rose Street; go across to it. In earlier times this street was well known to writers. The seventeenth-century poet Samuel Butler lived for many years, and died, in a house here. He's best known for a poem called "Hudibras." In 1679 the racy and highly successful playwright John Dryden was beaten up one night in Rose Street. Despite his sizable reward of £50 for information about who had organized the beating, he was never able to prove publicly who the culprit was. The usual suspect nowadays is the Earl of Rochester, who may have thought that Dryden had attacked him in print. But go into the passage to the right of the Lamb and Flag pub, which faces you in Rose Street, and you will see an inscription blaming the beating on Louise de Kéroüalle, who was an easy target for rumors. She was a mistress of King Charles, and very unpopular, being French and Catholic at a time when London was strongly nationalist and Protestant.

Notice the curled iron lamp-support high on the front of the pub. It now supports a flower basket in summer. The inside of the building shows how a lot of the best London pubs used to be before the modernization of the last few years. An old-fashioned strong beer (Director's) is served by hand pump. The sparse decor was common before brewers began trying hard to attract female customers. A wooden beam over the bar is decorated with a famous Medieval Latin poem in praise of liquor:

> *Meum est propositum in taberna mori;*
> *Vinum sit appositum morientis ori,*
> *Ut dicant, cum venerint, angelorum chori,*
> *"Deus sit propitius huic potatori."*

(The sign painter has got it almost right: the last vowel in *morientis* has been changed into a *u*. But it has been 1,500 years since sign painters around here got much practice in Latin.) The poem—in my translation—means:

To die in a pub is my definite plan,
With my mouth to the tap, just as close as I can.
Then the angels would say, when their singing began,
"O Lord, please show mercy to this boozy man."

In the eighteenth century there was another literary gent living in Rose Street—Edmund Curll, a publisher who specialized in erotic books. Several of Covent Garden's authors survived by writing steamy stuff for Mr. Curll. Curll was persecuted by the authorities, told off by the House of Lords, imprisoned and pilloried. (Being forced to stand in a pillory was serious punishment—you were an easy target for projectiles: litter, fruit and dead cats.)

Come back a few yards down Rose Street, following the sharp bend to the left as it joins King Street, which will lead you to the Central Market and the heart of Covent Garden. Just past the bend, on the left, is no. 27 King Street, the headquarters since 1812 of the Westminster Fire Office and its successor companies. Founded in 1717, the Westminster was one of the insurance firms that ran a private brigade of fire fighters. By crossing the street here, you can see, high on the front of the building, a very large and brightly painted molding of the Westminster's old badge. It shows a portcullis (a fortified screen for a castle gateway) crowned with three feathers. The three feathers are the traditional emblem of the Prince of Wales, the heir apparent to the throne. When the Westminster adopted them for its badge, it was with reference to the Prince of Wales who became King George II. George, who reigned from 1727 to 1760, was not one of Britain's most distinguished monarchs; his irreverent courtiers called him "Old Square-Toes." But he was one of the Westminster's earliest customers, and the company was proud to advertise that fact.

A hundred yards farther along, no. 43 King Street is the grandest surviving eighteenth-century house in Covent Garden. It has four stories and a flat front. On the second and third stories two pilasters with elaborate capitals divide the façade into three sections. The house was built in 1716–17 for Admiral Edward Rus-

Gaslight and a Lord High Admiral's House, Covent Garden

sell, Earl of Orford, a relative of the Russell family that owned Covent Garden. Russell was at that time one of the most powerful men in the country, and as Lord High Admiral had the enormous salary of £7,000 a year. He had become famous in 1692 as commander of the British fleet which defeated the French at the battle of La Hogue, off the coast of northern France; that defeat ended the hopes for a comeback of the Catholic King James II, who had lived under the protection of the French government since he had been driven from England in 1688. In Russell's great house here, the main dining room was on the first story, the master bedroom on the second, and the rooms of senior servants on the third.

Long after Russell's death, in 1856, a music hall called Evans's was built at the back of the house, and the management tried to make the place into a smart dining establishment. Music halls of the nineteenth and early-twentieth centuries are remembered now in Britain as jolly places in which liquor flowed plentifully but which were—like the modern pub—generally wholesome. This image, however, is a long way from the Victorian reality; Evans's had to battle to stay decent. Female customers were not welcome; they had to give their names and addresses upon entering, and were allowed to watch the performers only through a screen. These restrictions were meant to combat what Victorians called simply "the great social evil"—prostitution. From the seventeenth to the nineteenth century, Covent Garden swarmed with whores, and the music halls were one of their favorite "pitches." In at least one London music hall of the era the women used to do the whole of their business in the boxes. And one of the advertisements for Evans's virtually admitted that for a time whoredom had gained the upper hand here.

Opposite no. 43, 50 yards away across the flagstones, is the portico at the eastern end of St. Paul's Church. Like the rest of the church, it was built in the 1790s, following the earlier designs of Inigo Jones. In the Covent Garden that Jones constructed, similar colonnades were formed on the northern and eastern sides of the central rectangle, to harmonize with the portico here on the west. None of these original porticos remains, but you can see a nineteenth-century version of part of the northern portico adjoining Edward Russell's house. The open space, which made the piazza with its porticos a visible unity, has also gone, filled by the elegant Central Market of 1830.

In the church portico, notice the two gas lamps with reflectors mounted on massive iron brackets to match the grand scale of the portico itself. This spot has been a focus of Covent Garden events for centuries. In 1662, close to here, Samuel Pepys twice watched puppet shows. In the eighteenth century, Tom King's, a famous coffeehouse and brothel, stood against St. Paul's portico. King himself was a renegade member of the upper class; after his death, his widow, Moll King, became famous as the manager of the place. In 1739 the law caught up with her, charged her with keeping a disorderly house, and she spent some time in prison.

Later in the century there were rather more serious disorders here. The site was used for voting in parliamentary elections, and a wooden speaker's platform was built against the portico. Voting was done in public; people shouted threats and promises at the voters, and riots often developed. In 1784 the radical Charles James Fox was elected M.P. here after a wild campaign. His female supporters promenaded the streets with little replicas of foxtails as advertisements. At that time so few people were allowed to vote that it was possible to offer handsome inducements to those who could. Among Fox's women admirers were the attractive Duchess of Devonshire and her sister. These two ladies visited wavering voters in their homes, flattering and dazzling the men with their aristocratic charm. Rumors inevitably circulated about just how far they would go in revealing the attractions of voting for Fox.

During the riots at this election several people were killed. Gangs, which included impressively physical Irish coal-heavers and sedan-chair men, were organized to protect Fox and his supporters. (Sedan-chair men practiced their trade intensively at Covent Garden, waiting in long lines in the streets to be hired by people leaving the theaters; their chairs were miniature single-person carriages supported on long poles by two men, one in front and one behind. Sedan-chair men tended to be hefty, of course, and so were useful to hire for a riot.)

In more recent times St. Paul's portico has been the

setting of the opening scene of the musical *My Fair Lady* and of George Bernard Shaw's play *Pygmalion,* on which the former is based. Eliza Doolittle, a Cockney flower-seller, is trying to sell violets to wealthy people who crowd under the portico when it rains. Her accent is heard with interest by Henry Higgins, an expert on pronunciation; and he promises to convert her Cockney speech into upper-class diction within three months. In his play, Shaw, an Irishman, was satirizing English class divisions and the accents that helped to create them. He wrote in the introduction, "It is impossible for an Englishman to open his mouth without making some other Englishman hate or despise him."

Until the market workers moved away in 1974, Covent Garden remained famous for its social mixture. People in their finery from the opera drank in the same pubs as laborers from the market. And London pubs in general still seem to be more relaxed in this way than many in the provinces. (People going into a pub in the big city normally don't expect to come across acquaintances; perhaps this is why they seem less anxious to preserve social distinctions than people in smaller towns.)

Dickens, like Shaw, had fun with Cockney speech— the speech of nearly all working-class Londoners. Cockney continues to flourish today, though it has changed a little since Dickens's time. People no longer use *w* in place of *v* ("Werry good, sir") or add *h*'s in an attempt to be genteel. ("I do happreciate that.") In present-day Cockney, vowels are very different from those of BBC English, and consonants sometimes turn into vowels or disappear. In Cockney, the sentence "Here, put that in your mouth, will you?" would sound like "Eeya, pu de i yer mahf, wi-oo ya?"

Facing the portico of St. Paul's, about 50 yards east across the flagstones, is the Central Market, designed largely by the Georgian architect Charles Fowler. This building replaced the ramshackle collection of sheds and stalls that formed the market where the young Dickens had gazed at pineapples. For the market businesses, Fowler created a set of arcades running from east to west. At each end are columns and a triangular pediment, designed to match the roof and columns of

St. Paul's Church. The market now has great arched roofs, added in Victorian times.

Walk over to the market's southwest pavilion—the square building at the right-hand corner as you look out from the church portico. On the wall, in faded but distinct nineteenth-century lettering, is an advertisement for one of the firms that traded here: JA'S. BUTLER, HERBALIST & SEEDSMAN, LAVENDER WATER ETC. It is said that Mr. Butler specialized in selling hedgehogs. These animals, although flea-ridden, were kept in London homes because they ate beetles and cockroaches.

For over a century, the character of Covent Garden has been dictated by what happens in the Central Market. In the mid-nineteenth century the surrounding area teemed with fruit vendors, many of them immigrants speaking Irish Gaelic. A century later, the market trade clogged the neighboring streets with trucks, and tradespeople moved into many of the fine buildings around the market. Admiral Russell's house was taken over, and a great gash was made in its front to allow trucks access to the basement. In the late 1970s, after the market trade was removed, the Central Market remained unused. For perhaps the first time since the Middle Ages, the market and Covent Garden were quiet. Then, in 1980, the building reopened as an expensive shopping mall. The wealthy patrons it has attracted have created hopes of higher profits in the whole neighborhood. Rents have risen, and some of Covent Garden's traditional businesses, such as publishing houses and specialty shops, are moving away. But creative Covent Garden is regrouping around Neal Street, only a few hundred yards to the north.

For a while in the 1970s it seemed that the Central Market might be destroyed. A group in the Greater London Council—London's governing body—planned to demolish it and build lucrative offices in its place. Maiden Lane was also marked for destruction, to make way for a broad highway. Rule's restaurant and the gas lamps would have vanished, and Covent Garden in general would have ceased to be a pleasant place. But the plans were dropped—in the mid-1970s British property speculators ran short of money, fortunately.

Important opposition to these plans came from the

Covent Garden Community Association, (45 Shorts Gardens, WC2, tel. 836-3555), still an impressive alliance of long-term residents and young defenders of the area who fight to keep Covent Garden a place for craft workers and small, local independent businesses. The association has also worked to protect the housing in the area, lest Covent Garden become a lifeless quarter dominated by sleek office buildings and restaurants. Just to the south of the Central Market, the association helped to set up the delightful Jubilee Market, a flea market with prices that most locals *can* afford.

Head back toward Admiral Russell's house, and turn right to pass along the Victorian portico on the northern side of the Central Market. At the first corner, with James Street, is The Rock Garden, a restaurant with tables out under the portico in summer, and a cellar where bands blast away in the evenings. James Street is crossed by two more roads, Floral Street (gaslit) and Long Acre. On the corner with Long Acre is Covent Garden tube station; the fruit shop next to it boasts that it is the only greengrocery business to have stayed behind when the market moved in 1974.

However, I suggest not going up James Street on this walk. Cross it instead, and continue along the side of the Central Market. At the corner where the market ends is a small patch of open ground with stone seats and some inexpensive attempts at landscape gardening. On a sunny day you might find an occasional derelict lolling here. Locally, derelicts are called "dossers"; "to doss" means "to sleep rough." (There aren't very many of them in Covent Garden, but they are quietly valued by some of the more astute politicians in the community association: so long as dossers are in the area, fashionable and wealthy businesses may be reluctant to move their offices here.)

Twenty yards away, across Russell Street and facing the eastern end of the market, is Tutton's, which opened in 1977. Under the clever management of Jane Jones, this became one of the most pleasant of London's moderately priced restaurants. Previously, the building was a potato warehouse for the market; the present door frames were made from warehouse floor-

Tutton's

boards. When first constructed in 1887, the building was a hotel. You can see a faded mosaic from that era high on the wall at the end of the bar.

In several ways Tutton's is unusual by British standards. The tables on the sidewalk and the large windows allow customers to be entertained by watching the passersby in the French style. The sophisticated mixture of background music, alternating between baroque and soft-rock, would be hard to find outside Covent Garden. And the place transcends the rather rigid British distinctions between café, restaurant and pub. Cafés, serving tea, coffee and cakes, do their main business in the late morning and afternoon and normally close around five. Pubs in London close at 3:00 P.M. and do not open again until 5:30, and restaurants frequently don't come to life in the evening until about 7:00. This means that in many areas it's impossible to find refreshments in the early evening. Tutton's helps to solve this problem by offering the same menu from 9:00 in the morning until 11:30 at night. It is most crowded at lunchtime and in the late evening, when both drinks and food are served at the tables. I recommend going when it is less busy, in the morning or very early evening and especially around 5:30, when the bar reopens and the place glides from café to restaurant.

Perhaps without knowing it, Tutton's keeps up two local traditions. In the seventeenth century there was a Turkish bath on this site, where young men cleaned and revived themselves after an interlude in the brothels of nearby Drury Lane. The brothels have gone; they're now in Soho and Mayfair. But with the theaters and restaurants to attract revelers, there are still heavy nights to be had in Covent Garden. Breakfast at Tutton's afterwards aids a graceful recovery. In the eighteenth century, grand literary gents of Covent Garden used to hold court for hours and hours in the coffeehouses and clubs here in Russell Street. Nowadays the staff writers of the local publishing houses and advertising agencies act similarly, preening themselves a little as they sit conspicuously near the windows.

As you exit from the restaurant, you can see a long white building on your right, behind a patch of open ground: the Royal Opera House. Its grand entrance, with Corinthian columns, is on the side away to the right, in Bow Street. Perhaps the best-known musician to have used the Opera House is Handel, who in the 1730s had several oratorios premiered on this site. Today, the Opera House still sells some cheap tickets for its internationally renowned performances; lines of people form for hundreds of yards around the building. Many local residents stay away, thinking it mostly a place where wealthy tourists and the English upper class can glare at each other. The Opera House seems to have been rather more informal in the eighteenth and early-nineteenth centuries, when audiences rioted to demand seats at prices ordinary people could afford. One price rise at that time caused "continued hissing, groaning, howling, yelling, braying, barking and hooting . . . accompanied by exclamations of 'Old Prices,' 'No Rise,' 'No Private Boxes.' " On another occasion, an increase in prices incited the audience to smash the seats and chandeliers and to rip out the linings of the boxes. Fire was an even more serious threat, destroying early versions of the Opera House. The place was largely rebuilt in 1857–58; it is this version which remains.

About 30 yards along Russell Street notice the wine bar on the left. Perhaps the most striking thing about it is its name, Brahms and Liszt. The name does not honor the two composers; it's an off-color Cockney joke that is used publicly only because most people don't know, or don't like to admit that they know, what it means. Cockney speech has a code of rhyming slang, sometimes said to have started as a means of communicating so that the police could not understand. "Stairs," for example, were called "apples and pears," "corner" became "Johnnie Horner" and "to pinch" (meaning "to steal") became "to half-inch." "Brahms and Liszt" is rhyming slang for "pissed" (drunk).

Twenty yards farther on, Russell Street joins Bow Street and Wellington Street. On one corner is The Marquess of Anglesea, one of the most popular pubs in the district because it serves the traditional hand-pumped strong beer—Real Ale, as the enthusiasts call it. The brewery that supplies the pub is Young's, an evocative name for cognoscenti of London liquor: Young's is the only brewery in the capital to have completely refused to produce draught bitter beer that is

pasteurized and fizzy. Young's bitter is flat, contains living yeast, and is very strong.

Turn right at this crossroads, into Wellington Street. A few yards down on the right at no. 41 is Penhaligon's, a perfume shop and one of the best-known specialty businesses in London. Customers have included Sir Winston Churchill and the Duke of Edinburgh. In 1975 the first story of this late-nineteenth-century building was carefully reconstructed with antique furnishings as a Victorian shop. Its perfumes and toiletries, for men and women, are all made on the premises to the recipes of Walter Penhaligon, who founded the business in 1870. Pages of his handwritten notes are displayed on the wall of the shop. Between 10:00 and 12:00 on weekday mornings customers can watch through a glass screen as the perfumes are manufactured in a back room. On request, the perfumes are sold in antique bottles; customers can also bring their own favorite bottles to be filled. The toiletries and perfumes are not cheap. Unfortunately, the atmosphere in the shop seems to be slightly tense, perhaps a reflection of the exacting training and selection which the staff undergoes. Assistants who prove unsatisfactory are, I was told bluntly, "booted out." At times the service achieves an almost Parisian aloofness. The more skilled work—making the perfume—is done by a popular Cockney woman whose name I was not allowed to know.

Continue a few yards down Wellington Street, and take the first turn on the left into Tavistock Street. At the first corner on Tavistock Street you'll see the façade of the Theatre Royal, Drury Lane to the left. (Drury Lane itself runs past the back of the building.) The theater began its life in 1663, shortly after the restoration of King Charles II; the "Royal" in its title refers to him. Like the Opera House, it has twice been destroyed by fire, with the second great blaze occurring in 1809, when the playwright Richard Brinsley Sheridan was manager. The building at that time was drastically underinsured. The story goes that when Sheridan realized that the theater was well alight, he knew immediately that he was ruined and did not rush about trying to save things. Instead, he settled down

Wine bar with coded message in name

with a bottle of wine at a nearby tavern to watch the blaze. When someone asked him why he wasn't making any effort to help the burning theater, he replied, "Cannot a man enjoy a glass of wine by his own fireside?"

The present building was erected in 1811–12. This is the only theater in London to have Georgian sections remaining in its interior—two grand staircases and the rotunda to which they lead. Perhaps the most pleasant part of the theater's exterior is the long colonnade on the north side. You can see it by walking a few yards up Catherine Street, past the theater entrance, and turning right into Russell Street. The colonnade was added to the building in 1831–32, early in the reign of King William IV. Its Ionic columns are of cast iron; between them, in delicate, looping brackets, are large gas lamps.

Enter the colonnade and walk about 15 yards. Here, about 14 feet up on the theater wall, you can see signs of the precautions taken when the building was new to prevent yet another ruinous fire; next to each other, and easily missed, are two metal fire marks with initials showing that they belonged to two local insurance companies—St. Martin's and St. Paul's Covent Garden.

Perhaps the best-known person to have acted at the Theatre Royal is Nell Gwynne, a clever but illiterate woman who began her career at Drury Lane in the 1660s by selling oranges—and perhaps herself. Samuel Pepys describes happily that he kissed Nell, an ample redhead; Pepys's wife kissed her too, though no doubt with rather less enthusiasm. For a time, Pepys enjoyed hearing stories of Nell's razor tongue. But Nell came to the attention of King Charles II, who made her his mistress, and Pepys, disappointed, lost interest in her. Later, when he found himself in the box next to hers at the theater, he described sourly how "that jade Nell . . . lay there laughing upon the people."

A Protestant, Nell seems to have become popular with the London crowds, who thought of her as a rival to the King's Catholic mistress, Louise de Kéroüalle. A story is told that one day a crowd caught sight of a grand carriage with Nell inside, but mistakenly assumed that it was the hated Louise. Insults flew until

Penhaligon's perfumes

Nell appeared at the carriage window and called out with an actress' poise, "Pray, good people, be civil; it is the *Protestant* whore."

In England, Nell Gwynne is almost a household name. She was succeeded at the Drury Lane theater by a woman of great wit and accomplishment who is now almost entirely forgotten. This woman spent many years in Covent Garden, and the story of her wild and sad life will end this walk.

Her name was Charlotte Charke. She was born about 1710, the daughter of the highly successful actor and dramatist Colley Cibber. Interestingly, Cibber gave his daughter a liberal education; Charlotte later wrote that it "might have been sufficient for a son instead of a daughter. . . . I was never made much acquainted with a needle, which I handle with the same clumsy awkwardness a monkey does a kitten." Instead, she was taught Italian and Latin. At fourteen, she became a good shot; then a fussy woman neighbor complained that this was unfeminine. "Upon this sober lady's hint, I was deprived of my gun; and with a half-broken heart on the occasion, resolved to revenge myself, by getting a muscatoon [a type of musket] that hung over the kitchen mantelpiece, and use my utmost endeavours towards shooting down her chimneys."

Later in her teens, Charlotte used her education and social position to set herself up as a quack doctor. She afterwards admitted that she had been dreadfully ignorant of medicine. But "this defect was not discovered by my patients, as I put on significancy of countenance [a knowing air] that served to convince them of my incomparable skill and abilities." One day when she ran out of drugs she got an urgent request for medicine from an old woman. Something harmless but revolting was obviously required, to make the patient feel that it *must* be doing her good. So Charlotte collected and boiled a large number of snails, and sold the result as medicine. The old woman later returned with an eager account of the "medicine's" success, and demanded more. Charlotte noted acutely that the success of many physicians "is rather founded on the faith of the patient, than any real merit in the doctor or his prescriptions."

She married young. Her husband was a violinist,

and Charlotte came to suspect that he had married her to exploit her father's influence at the Drury Lane theater. Her own motive for marrying was little better: "I thought it gave me an air of more consequence to be called Mrs. Charke than Miss Charlotte." The marriage did not last long. According to Charlotte, her husband sponged off her for money and chased after the public women of Covent Garden—"common wretches that were to be had for half a crown!" (Half a crown, incidentally, was not a trivial sum; in the 1880s prostitutes in London's rough East End were asking only a fifth of that—sixpence.)

Charlotte herself became an actress at the Drury Lane theater, and when her name first appeared in the theater's advertisements she went around London excitedly for days, gazing at them. But in 1735 she fell out with the manager at Drury Lane, a Mr. Fletewood. Feeling wronged, she retaliated by writing a play satirizing Fletewood—and herself. It was called *The Art of Management*, and seems to have been performed at least once, with Charlotte acting "herself" under the ironic (and prophetic) name of "Mrs. Tragic." Fletewood was so embarrassed that he bought up almost every printed copy of the play to prevent the public from reading it. The crumbling copy now in the library of the British Museum is one of the very few to have survived.

Charlotte's pride led to quarrels with her family. Staying with her sister once, she was given a bedroom that proved cold and leaky. She took her revenge by composing doggerel verses about the room. Criticizing the bedclothes, she wrote:

> So charming thin, the darns so neat,
> With great conveniency expel the heat.

She also quarreled with her father, who refused to see her. When she pleaded for reconciliation, he returned her letter unopened. Charlotte's revenge this time was to publish the letter—which, of course, made reconciliation even more unlikely. She denied a rumor that she had publicly slapped her father in the face with a fish. She also denied the story that, dressed as a highwaywoman with pistols, she once held up her father on the outskirts of London and robbed him of more than £60.

Charlotte seems to have been very fond of her only child, Kitty. Rejected by her family, and finding it difficult to get work as an actress, she had a hard time providing for herself and the child. At one point she tried retailing in Covent Garden: "I took it into my head to dive into TRADE. To that end, I took a shop in Long Acre, and turned oil-woman and grocer." Here she sold links for escorting coaches and sedan chairs at night. One link boy visited her shop "just before candle time, which is the dusky part of the evening, the most convenient light for perpetrating a wicked intent," and stole all her brass weights. She didn't meet him again—until one day when she caught sight of him in a cart being taken to Tyburn to be hanged.

For a time Charlotte worked as a waitress, which meant walking every night across the fields to the northwest part of Covent Garden where thieves—called footpads—flourished. She later wrote dryly, "I have often wondered I have escaped without wounds or blows from the gentlemen of the pad, who are numerous and frequent in their evening patrols through them fields, and my march extended as far as Long Acre, by which means I was obliged to pass through the thickest of 'em." Nonhuman thieves were a menace, too. Charlotte sold sausages, until a dog intervened: "Oh! DISASTROUS CHANCE! A hungry cur most savagely entered my apartment . . . and most inconsiderately devoured my remaining stock."

Faced with a grave lack of money, she was congratulated by her friends for refusing to do what innumerable women did in her position—go onto the streets. Her debts grew, and she had the terrifying experience of being put into a debtors' prison, where people could rot away for years. When released, she tried to evade her creditors by living disguised as a man. She made a good-looking man, and got an offer of marriage from an heiress. Charlotte has written wistfully about how she could have made a fortune if she had only been willing to pose as a man and marry her.

She worked for a while with a troupe of traveling actors, and was briefly locked up in prison in the west of England—"among the felons, whose chains were rattling all night long, and made the most hideous noise I ever heard, there being upwards of two hundred men and boys under the different sentences of death and transportation."

In 1755 Charlotte published an autobiography; it's delightfully written in a tough, self-mocking style. She called the book "some account of my unaccountable life," and described it as "this little brat of my brain." Nearly all the above quotations are taken from it.* Though the book had some success when it first appeared (it went into two editions), it did not make Charlotte Charke's fortune. On the last occasion that we hear of this brave and talented Covent Garden character, she was growing old in poverty, with only a dog and a pet magpie for company.

A Narrative of the Life of Mrs. Charlotte Charke, introduction by L. R. N. Ashley (Gainesville, Fla.: Scholars' Facsimiles and Reprints, 1969).

Walk

2

Legal and Illegal London: The Inns of Court

This walk will take in three of the four Inns of Court: Lincoln's Inn, the Inner Temple and the Middle Temple. This is perhaps the prettiest and most historical of our walks, with fewer pubs and shops than in other parts of London. One note of warning: Lincoln's Inn doesn't allow visitors on weekends. So this is a walk best done on a weekday.

The Inns of Court were formed in the Middle Ages, and were called Inns because they gave lodging to lawyers, legal students and others in search of smart company. Until the eighteenth century, the Inns were like universities of law; sometimes there were student disturbances of a colorful and still-familiar kind. Today with their quiet courtyards, and chambers arranged around open staircases, the Inns feel very much like Oxford or Cambridge colleges. The Inns are in the middle of town, near the boundary between the ancient cities of London and Westminster, and about half a mile east of Covent Garden. (The fourth Inn, Gray's, not on today's route, is nearby.) Their rows of fine seventeenth- and eighteenth-century buildings are fairly well hidden from the outside. People who have lived in London for years often say, when shown the Inns, that they never realized they were there.

Today the Inns are not the main centers of legal education, and students no longer live in them. The chambers in the Inns have become extremely valuable; the rent is far beyond the means of most students. They are occupied mostly by practicing barristers and solicitors—the two kinds of English lawyer. (In outline, barristers have a virtual monopoly on professional pleading in the higher courts: solicitors do the primary research into legal cases and then instruct, or "brief," barristers to represent clients in court.)

The Inns are controlled by barristers, the more glamorous kind of lawyer. In court a barrister still wears a long black gown and a gray wig. A person in this austere costume, delivering a speech of well-

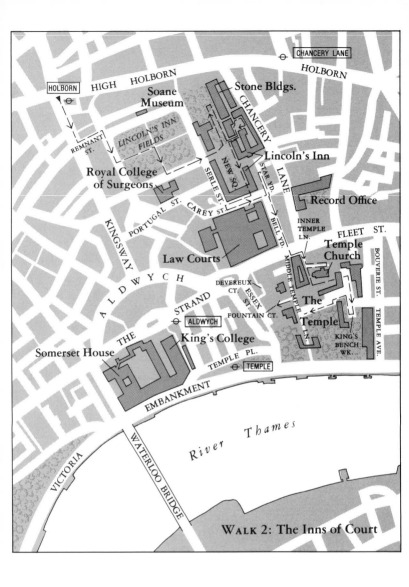

WALK 2: The Inns of Court

rehearsed aggression, is a dramatic sight in a paneled courtroom—as barristers themselves are well aware. The main English civil courts are close to the route of our walk, and if you go through the Inns on a day in legal term (the main legal vacation occurs in August and September), you'll probably see barristers in their grand dress, walking between their chambers and the courts.

Although the Inns are now used mainly for lawyers'

offices, legal students still come here when qualifying as barristers. Only by being affiliated with one of the four Inns of Court, and by passing exams set jointly by them, can a person become a barrister. Each Inn insists that its students attend a number of dinners in its hall. "Eating dinners," in the lawyers' phrase, is a student's introduction to the legal community, and this is done partly to preserve tradition and to foster camaraderie. Clients sometimes find this professional solidarity rather chilling, but the lawyers usually have more in common with one another than with the clients, and are anxious not to quarrel with their colleagues.

Each Inn is an independent body, governed by a group of its judges and senior barristers who are called Benchers (strictly, Masters of the Bench); this group serves under an annually elected official, the Treasurer. Quarrels sometimes occur between the Inns. In 1882 there was a splendidly petty wrangle when the Treasurers of the four Inns decided to send a joint declaration of loyalty to Queen Victoria. The plan almost fell through because the Treasurers disagreed as to whose signature was to appear first on the declaration. Eventually they compromised; the document was presented not by the Treasurers but by the Queen's son, Prince Edward, acting for the Inns. Even so, local chauvinism remained: a historian of the Middle Temple noted slyly that Edward was "himself a member of *our* Bench."

On the way to the Inns you will walk through Lincoln's Inn Fields, now a park set with towering plane trees, but once the site of some of England's most sensational executions. The grand buildings around the Fields have some sinister tales of their own; perhaps most tragic of all, as we shall see at the end of the walk, is the story of the medieval Templar knights, who have given their name to the site of the Inner and the Middle Temple.

At the chief exit from Holborn tube station, turn left onto the main road, Kingsway. From Kingsway, take the third little entrance on the left, Remnant Street. Where Remnant Street ends, about 60 yards away, turn right and see Lincoln's Inn Fields. Pass along the Fields for a few yards, keeping them on your left and the row of grand houses on your right.

The sixth of these houses, no. 59–60, was once among the most fashionable in London. It was built about 1640, possibly by the best-known architect of the time, Inigo Jones. Behind the tall windows on the second story were the finest rooms. The pilasters (inset columns) rising between the windows gave the building the desired Italian appearance; look carefully and you will see that they narrow toward the top. The architectural term for this is *entasis*; it was used for the columns of Greek temples, including the Parthenon, because perfectly straight columns gave an optical illusion of splaying at the top, and could make a building appear squat.

This house has had some noted occupants. In 1664 it was bought by an eccentric Protestant aristocrat, Charles Powlett, who lived here for over twenty years. Powlett was Marquis of Winchester in 1685 when a Catholic king, James II, came to the throne; to avoid the dangerous choice between supporting or opposing the King, he pretended to be mad. He drove around the country with a procession of coaches and a huge troop of horsemen, sleeping during the daytime and giving wild parties at night. Luckily for his finances, this act became unnecessary after three years, when James II was deposed. Powlett got his reward from the incoming Protestant rulers, William III and his wife, Mary: he was promoted to Duke.

In 1683 Powlett's house had been used for a grisly purpose—fitting together the body and severed head of Lord William Russell, another Protestant, who had just been executed for high treason in Lincoln's Inn Fields. Russell was believed to have been plotting to kill King Charles II and his Catholic brother, James, for fear that James would shortly come to the throne. Powlett probably sympathized with his unlucky fellow aristocrat, and offered his house for this preliminary to burial. Later, William and Mary tried to compensate Russell's family by making his father, the Earl of Bedford, a duke. (The Earl owned Covent Garden, so this was how the landlords of that area became dukes.)

In 1700 another colorful nobleman lived in this house: Charles Sackville, Earl of Dorset. Earlier in his life Sackville had been involved in indecent exposure, robbery and murder. Samuel Pepys mentioned in his diary that Sackville fought and was imprisoned after "running up and down all the night almost naked through the streets." Sackville was also the lover of Nell Gwynne before she became famous as the mistress of Charles II. Later Nell is said to have called Charles Sackville "my Charles the First." At the time, he was not yet Earl of Dorset, but had the title Lord Buckhurst. Pepys noted that Nell was insulted one day by a rival actress, Beck Marshall, who called her "Lord Buckhurst's whore." Nell replied that she was only one man's whore, although she had been brought up in a brothel; Beck, she said, had been brought up the daughter of a pious chapel-goer but she was now the whore of several!

Sackville was followed by yet another aristocrat, Robert Bertie, 4th Earl of Lindsey, from whom the building gets its present name, Lindsey House. In 1791 the house got its most famous resident of all. By looking through the railings outside the house, you can see a plaque to the right of the entrance dedicated to him: Spencer Perceval, the only British Prime Minister to have been assassinated.

Perceval was the second son of an earl; inheriting less than he desired, he became a barrister and also found a sinecure—such posts flourished around 1800. Perceval's sinecure was at the Royal Mint; he was "surveyor of the meltings and clerk of the irons," and the income helped him to afford Lindsey House. In 1792 Perceval was employed by the government to prosecute Tom Paine, the radical supporter of the American and French revolutions and author of *Common Sense* and *The Rights of Man*. By 1803, while still living here, Perceval was Attorney General and the prosecutor of another famous radical, Colonel Despard. Despard, unlike Paine, was actually in the hands of the government when tried, and his prosecution caused a sensation.

Despard was an Irishman with a good war record. But after his success at soldiering, he had been disappointed with his treatment by the government, and he had turned to radicalism. In 1802 he was charged with plotting to kill the King, the frequently insane George III. A witness called by Perceval said that Despard had suggested firing a cannon at the King as he traveled in a coach to Parliament. The prosecution was successful; the jury voted "guilty" but strongly recommended mercy for the distinguished ex-soldier. The judge had other ideas. At the time, the rich in Britain were terrified that the French Revolution would cross the Channel. Radicals were making jokes about chopping up the nobility and turning them into "aristocrat pies." Despard, said the judge, had proposed "instead of the ancient limited monarchy of this realm . . . its useful gradations of rank, its natural and inevitable, as well as desirable inequalities of property, to substitute a wild scheme of impracticable equality"—the *égalité* of the French Revolution. Despard and associates were sentenced to hang.

With a rope around his neck, Despard was allowed to make a short speech from the scaffold to the crowd of onlookers, though he was warned that the trap would be dropped the moment he said "an inflammatory or improper word." After he had spoken briefly about despotism and his being a friend of the poor, he was stopped, and the execution took place. Two of those hanged with him didn't die quickly enough; the executioner had to tug at their legs to speed things up.

After this success in prosecuting Despard, Spencer Perceval lived for another nine years. To his credit, he did help reduce the evils of the slave trade, and he refused to prosecute the early organizers of British labor unions. In 1808 he moved from the house in Lincoln's Inn Fields to one on Downing Street. The next year he became Prime Minister. On May 11, 1812, a failed businessman named John Bellingham, with a grievance against the government, waited for Perceval in the House of Commons and shot him in the chest with a pistol. Perceval died. Bellingham was hanged a week later.

Before leaving this old house, look at the three rusting iron brackets above the railings at the front. They date from the days before gas lighting, from the eighteenth century. Inside the brackets were globes of glass, each containing an oil lamp with reservoir and wick; below each bracket is a short horizontal bar, where the lamplighter rested his ladder. In the eighteenth century, the unlit fields across the road were alive with criminals at night, and the residents of the great houses hoped that such oil lights would keep them away.

John Gay, a poet of the 1720s, knew these fields

well and wrote verses advising travelers how to avoid being robbed here. They should stick to the oil-lit streets, he said, and not be tempted to hire a link man to escort them with blazing torch across the fields. Link men deliberately led travelers into ambushes, and then took a share of the spoils:

> Where Lincoln's Inn, wide space, is railed around,
> Cross not with venturous step; there oft is found
> The lurking thief . . .
> Though thou art tempted by the link-man's call,
> Yet trust him not along the lonely wall;
> In the mid way he'll quench the flaming brand,
> And share the booty with the pilfering band.
> Still keep the public streets, where oily rays,
> Shot from the crystal lamp, o'erspread the ways . . .

Next door is another grand residence, nos. 57–58 Lincoln's Inn Fields. It was built in 1730 to harmonize with Lindsey House, and has similar pilasters and tall windows. For most of this century the place has housed a firm of solicitors, Marks and Clerk; you can see their worn brass plate on an inner door. In front is a yard of pleasant flagstones, empty on weekends and open to the road, but I don't advise walking onto it. Once when I did, an angry gentleman told me about legal rights, saying "How would you like trespassers in *your* back garden?" This isn't a back garden, of course, and legal rights may be different from moral rights. But on weekdays it may be best to view the house from the road.

In the mid-1780s, this was the town house of a well-known lawyer, Lord Chief Justice Mansfield. In the previous decade Mansfield had lived a little northwest of here, in Bloomsbury, but his house there had been burned down in 1780 by a rioting Protestant crowd, angry at his liberal policy towards Catholics. (More later about these rioters, many of whom were eventually shot.) Mansfield found his house in Lincoln's Inn Fields a more peaceful place. In 1788 he retired from here to Kenwood House, a mansion in Hampstead.

In the 1790s, the building here was divided: the graceful porch with its classical columns was installed by a leading architect, John Soane, in an attempt to distract attention from the new and demeaning double doors. The section on the right, no. 58, became well known to Charles Dickens, because from 1834 to 1856 this was the home of his friend and biographer John Forster. Dickens mentioned the place in *Bleak House*, imagining it as the home of the secretive lawyer Tulkinghorn, whose eventual murder in the house is described with enthusiasm.

On December 2, 1844, Dickens came to no. 58 to give a private reading of "The Chimes," a tearful story about the poor. One of the people in his small audience did a satirical drawing of the occasion: it shows two of the male listeners apparently weeping; the host, Forster, sitting apelike in the foreground; and the divine Dickens reading with a supernatural light radiating from his head.

The reading was such a success that he was persuaded to repeat the performance three days later. These may have been Dickens's first dramatic readings from his work; years later, similar readings to large audiences were to kill him. There was a huge demand for such readings; by his late forties Dickens was desperately overworked, and his portraits show a ravaged, weary face. He was already wealthy but remained anxious for money. In deciding to give a tour of readings in the United States when he was in his mid-fifties, he admitted that the "likelihood of making a very great addition to my capital in half a year" was "an immense consideration." He made nearly £20,000 (a huge amount in those days) in America. In New York people spent large sums simply to buy places in line for the readings. Back in England, Dickens, against medical advice, took on even more readings, collapsed and died.

Cross the road directly opposite no. 58, and take the path into the park, Lincoln's Inn Fields proper. One hundred yards' walk will bring you to the park's center, a space canopied by plane trees surrounding a wooden pavilion. Marked out in the shade here are two netball courts, used at lunchtime by young women from the nearby offices. Netball is rather like basketball, and in Britain is played almost exclusively by women; but the spectators who gather here at midday to watch the short-skirted players are almost all men.

The outer fields are much used in summer for eating, sunbathing and courting. In earlier times they were less attractive. In 1735 an Act of Parliament reported that "the great square ... Lincoln's Inn Fields ... hath for some years past lain waste and in great disorder, whereby the same has become a receptacle for rubbish, dirt and nastiness of all sorts." The Act went on about "robberies, assaults, outrages and enormities" which happened here. One incident in the 1730s involved a senior legal official, Sir Joseph Jekyll, who had promoted a law which put a tax on liquor of £1 per gallon; drinkers retaliated by beating him up in Lincoln's Inn Fields. The government then had to provide Jekyll with a guard of sixty soldiers. His law was known as the "gin act," gin (mixed with fruit juice) being the great opiate of the eighteenth-century English masses. William Hogarth, an artist of the time, produced famous paintings of the horrors of gin drinking; some of his original work can now be seen in Lincoln's Inn Fields at the Soane Museum. (Though the museum isn't part of the walk today, you could reach it by turning left at the wooden pavilion, and leaving the park by the path which then faces you. The museum specializes in interior furnishings, and is at no. 13, Lincoln's Inn Fields.)

The grim fields were a suitable place for well-attended executions. In 1586, fourteen men were convicted of plotting to kill Protestant Elizabeth I, and of attempting to put on the throne her Catholic cousin, Mary Queen of Scots. They were executed here, some of them by a barbaric procedure—hanging, drawing and quartering—which meant being hanged for a short time, castrated, disemboweled while alive, chopped into quarters and beheaded. Quartering allowed parts of the victim to be publicly displayed in several places, a warning to as many subjects as possible of the dangers of plotting against the sovereign. Great care was taken with the quarters and severed heads; after the execution they were boiled in the hangman's cauldron to preserve them and to make them less palatable to birds.

One of the plotters of 1586, Anthony Babington, showed a striking composure during the execution here. His fellow convicts knelt in prayer, but Babington stood with his hat on and calmly watched the executioner's knife do to the first victim what it was shortly to do to him. Mary Queen of Scots had written earlier to encourage Babington in his plot, and it was this which gave Queen Elizabeth's government its public justification for beheading Mary herself in the following year.

Turn right at the pavilion, and the path will take you out of the park to a spot where you will encounter a vast classical structure. This is the façade of the Royal College of Surgeons—pompous, and probably meant to be. The college sets examinations in surgery; lectures and experiments are also held here. Today surgeons in England have, of course, a flawless reputation (save for the occasional one who mistakenly sews up an instrument inside a living patient). But this good name has not always existed. In the early nineteenth century surgeons performed grim and clumsy operations, and sometimes had characters to match. Needing fresh corpses to dissect, some surgeons of the time were notorious for their links with the "resurrectionists"—men who illegally dug up the dead for sale as medical specimens. When, in the 1840s, Florence Nightingale told her grand and wealthy parents that she wished to practice nursing, they could not at first understand. The nurses of the day were, as one authority put it, "without exception drunkards." At last her mother thought she had the explanation: Florence must be in love "with a low, vulgar surgeon."

The surgeons' impressive building here, mostly built in the 1830s, was designed by a fashionable architect, Charles Barry (he also designed the present Houses of Parliament). Barry was almost certainly trying to improve the surgeons' unfortunate image by making them a splendid and dignified headquarters. Notice the vast columns at the front, surmounted by ramshorn curls ("Ionic volutes," in architects' jargon). Horrifying medical practices went on for some time after the 1830s. John Hall, a senior military physician during the Crimean War of the 1850s, refused to let his surgeons use the new anesthetic, chloroform. Instead, amputations had to be carried out on fully conscious patients, sometimes by moonlight. Charles Barry's vast building stands as an overwhelming tomb, a memorial to the bad old days of English surgery.

As you leave the park, turn left onto the sidewalk, and 100 yards ahead you will see a large, arched gate-

Gaslight at Lincoln's Inn

way. Go through it (unless it's Saturday or Sunday), and you are inside Lincoln's Inn.

The Inn has been here since before 1422; its surviving records begin in that year, but the place had obviously been flourishing earlier. The name Lincoln is rather mysterious; it may have come from a medieval Earl of Lincoln who had a house nearby. The oldest building to be seen nowadays is the Old Hall, built in 1489 of red brick; you can see it from the entrance, 100 yards straight ahead between the trees. You'll reach it in a few minutes; first, though, go 10 yards inside the entrance and look left at the hefty door set in the wall and studded with iron. This is part of a Victorian upstairs-downstairs arrangement. The door leads to a steep flight of steps which descend to the kitchens of the Inn. Look up and you will see the end of the hall where the lawyers dine—upstairs. The architecture of the hall resembles that of around 1600. You will see the building from a better angle in a moment, but from here you can see its true date, confessed in blue brick above the great window, 1843. Also in blue brick are the initials of the architect: P. H. (Philip Hardwick).

Go 20 yards beyond the kitchen doorway, and turn left up the first flight of steps. Where these steps themselves turn left you'll see an ornamented water tank made of lead. In summer it is overhung by flowering fuchsias; part these, and see the date molded into the metal: 1685. (There will be something to say later about this eventful year, in which Charles II died and was succeeded, with much bloodshed, by his brother James.) The steps here lead to the entrance of the hall, and have metal fixtures for carpet rods. Since the steps are outdoors, a carpet can be laid only on rare occasions, such as a royal visit.

At the top of the steps on the left you get a good view of the hall where trainee barristers "eat their dinners" in the company of their seniors. Notice the intricate decoration in the imitation-Tudor design on the tall chimney pots and the two-storied cupola on the roof, equipped with its own miniature flying buttresses.

Go along the gravel to the far end of the hall, where the library of the Inn juts out at a right angle. Just to the left of the library steps is another antique water tank; the design shows cherubs pulling a chariot. High on the library wall, to the right of the steps, is a coat of arms with an appropriate legal motto in rhyming Latin: *Pro rege, lege, grege*—"On behalf of the king, the law and the herd," in that order.

Go down the steps on the right, and a few yards ahead of you will be a little nineteenth-century hut built of brick. Ten feet tall and 7 feet wide, it is crowned by pinnacles and has a pointed Gothic arch over the door. It is used to store garden tools, and has been called the "Head Gardener's Castle." The architect, George Gilbert Scott, also built the large and serious set of legal chambers behind it. He was, to put it mildly, a Gothic enthusiast, and even the little hut needed its formal Gothic decoration. I was told that earlier in this century the hut was used as a den by an eminent lawyer. It seems to have been designed originally for the servant who looked after the horses and carriages of visitors. Outside the hut the drive widens into a large rectangle: here the servant turned the carriages around, to be ready for departure.

Just beyond the Gardener's Castle is the start of a long stone eighteenth-century building. Two-thirds of the way along its façade is a fine sundial, decorated in blue and gold. For a better view of it, go a few yards up the path that winds away to the left into the garden of the Inn. The inscription on the sundial reads:

T
Rt. Hon.
W. P.
1794

The large "T" stands for Treasurer of the Inn; "Rt. Hon." (Right Honourable) means that the Treasurer commemorated here was a member of the Privy Council, a senior body of state; "W. P." are his initials—William Pitt, who was at the time Prime Minister.

Pitt was in several ways a striking man. He had become Prime Minister at the age of twenty-four—his father had been Prime Minister, which helped. When the news of the young Pitt's appointment was given to the House of Commons, it was met with a howl of laughter. As Prime Minister, Pitt opposed the revolutionary French overseas, and tried to crush radicals at home who sympathized with France. The radicals retaliated with abuse and satire. It was pointed out that Pitt spent curiously little time with women; as one wit naughtily put it, referring to Britain personified as the lady Britannia, Pitt wasn't fit to stand at Britannia's head if he couldn't stand at her tail. Pitt was, however, tempted by liquor, especially port. He entered the House of Commons one day dead drunk, with his friend Henry (Hal) Dundas, who was in a similar state—too drunk, perhaps, to make out the Speaker of the House. The incident became famous; an eminent scholar of the time wrote a parody:

> PITT: I can't discern the Speaker, Hal; can you?
> DUNDAS: Not see the Speaker! Damn me, I see two.

Pitt died at forty-six, after an effective career as a Conservative. Parliament arranged to pay his debts of £40,000.

Several other British Prime Ministers have qualified as barristers at Lincoln's Inn, including the great nineteenth-century rivals, Disraeli and Gladstone. (It was Disraeli who shrewdly bought a large British holding in the Suez Canal Company, highly profitable before 1956.) In the early 1950s Mrs. Margaret Hilda Thatcher "ate dinners" here, after some years as a research chemist at Oxford.

At the far end of the lawn facing Pitt's sundial you may see, in summer, metal hoops set up for the gentle and skilled game of croquet. At lunchtime the public is allowed to go right along the path by this lawn. When you walk back, keep the Gardener's Castle on your left and the mock-Tudor hall on your right; on reaching the road that runs from the main entrance of the Inn, turn left and walk the 50 yards to the place where the chapel and Old Hall join. The chapel, on the left, has been largely rebuilt in this century; it was one of the few London buildings to be bombed in the First World War. (The bombing at that time caused such panic that in the 1930s many expected London's morale to collapse within days if there were ever to be a second war with Germany.) The previous chapel was built in the 1620s on stone piers, which are still standing; go through the chapel entrance, and walk in the

Head gardener and his Victorian hut,
Lincoln's Inn

undercroft between the piers. This cold but dry space underneath the chapel once served as a rendezvous. Samuel Pepys mentions meeting an acquaintance here in 1663. Set in the floor are gravestones, many of them made unreadable through wear. Go to the central pier; two feet from it, to the left, you can still make out the name on the gravestone of John Thurloe, secretary of state in the 1650s, during the short era when England was a republic. As the assistant of Oliver Cromwell, Thurloe ran a superb spy network which penetrated the court of the exiled Charles II. After Cromwell's death and Charles's return to England, Thurloe may have expected to be executed, as other prominent republicans were. But he was spared, perhaps because, as a spymaster, he knew too much about some of the King's Cavalier supporters who had been playing a double game. (Thurloe is supposed to have said that, if he were hanged, he had a "black book" which would hang many who now claimed to be loyal Cavaliers.) Thurloe retired from politics in 1660; within a few years even royalists were complaining publicly that the nation's spies weren't nearly as efficient as they had been during the republic under Thurloe's management.

Leave the undercroft by its open right side, and you'll come into a delightful little gaslit court. The brick building to your right, adjoining the chapel, is the Old Hall, the fifteenth-century structure which you saw earlier from a distance. From 1737 to 1875 this was where the High Court of Chancery met outside legal term. The High Court heard some of the most important disputes over property, and Dickens opened *Bleak House* in this setting. Dickens disliked lawyers; he may have considered them fellows of the legal men who had helped to imprison his own father for debt in the 1820s and 1830s. In *Bleak House* he tried to convey how dismal the High Court was:

> London. Michaelmas Term lately over. . . . Implacable November weather. . . . Fog everywhere. Fog up the river . . . fog down the river. . . . And hard by Temple Bar, in Lincoln's Inn Hall, at the very heart of the fog, sits the Lord High Chancellor in his High Court of Chancery. . . .

The fog symbolizes the obscurity of the law; all

through the novel the property dispute of *Jarndyce* v. *Jarndyce* drags on. By the time the case is solved, no property is left—the whole estate has been used in paying lawyers' bills. Dickens based the Jarndyce affair on a real legal case; he was attacking "Chancery abuses and delays." Even today, costs in the reformed High Court can be vast. In 1979 the costs of a five-day libel hearing awarded against the plaintiff (a journalist) were estimated at £20,000. Although Chancery cases are no longer heard within Lincoln's Inn, the lawyers here still specialize in work of this kind; criminal lawyers are more likely to be found in the other three Inns.

In 1698 the Old Hall was the scene of a strange legal episode concerning the will of Dr. Nicholas Barbon, a speculative builder who may well have erected New Square (a large and fine courtyard of Lincoln's Inn which you will reach in a moment). Barbon was a ruthless character, known for overriding the opposition to his building projects with an aristocratic blend of insensitivity and glamour. He decided that, even from the grave, he would go on defeating people: he wrote in his will that his creditors should never be paid, and to execute the will he chose John Asgill, a lawyer from Lincoln's Inn. After Barbon's death, Asgill called a meeting at the Old Hall. The creditors appeared, no doubt expecting, in the modern lawyers' phrase, "to learn something to their advantage." Asgill read the will, including the part about nonpayment of debts, and then told the appalled creditors, "Gentlemen, you have heard the Doctor's testament: I assure you, I will religiously attend to the wishes of the deceased." A stylish affront, of which Barbon himself might have been proud.

John Asgill was an interesting character in his own right; among other things, he published a book which argued that death was an illusion. Asgill claimed that if God respected the principles of English law—and surely He must!—then, after Christ's sacrifice, He could no longer oblige Christians to die. Instead, at the end of their lives they were "translated" into another existence. Asgill may have intended the book to be a satire; but in any case, the Irish House of Commons ordered it to be burned. After failing in some financial schemes, Asgill spent his last years in a debtors' prison, no doubt to the satisfaction of any of Barbon's surviving creditors.

Walk through the covered passage between the chapel and the Old Hall, noticing the timber set into the brickwork. Ahead of you and to the left is now the garden of New Square, overlooked on three sides by late-seventeenth-century buildings which are possibly the results of Barbon's scheming. The intricate iron gates which led into the garden are still in place, close to the road leading to the Inn's entrance; they bear the date 1863. Until the Second World War the gates were connected with iron railings around the garden, but now most of the railings have gone and the locks of the gates, unused, have largely rusted away. During the war, ornamental iron railings like these were cut down by government order. Officially, the commandeered metal was to be reused for making weapons. But rumors circulated that many railings passed the war peacefully in huge unused dumps, and that the main effect of requisitioning them had been to give the impression that the government was doing something useful.

The gardens of Lincoln's Inn now stretch from New Square up past the Gardener's Castle to the stone building, several hundred yards away. In the Middle Ages part of the gardens (the section which now faces Pitt's sundial) was called the Coneygarth, the rabbit garden. The rabbits made a good target for hungry or clowning legal students, and the Inn had to make a rule forbidding the young gentlemen to shoot arrows at them. In 1489, the time when the Old Hall was built, the Benchers of the Inn also set a fine (twenty shillings) for any member caught fornicating in the Coneygarth. No doubt because detection was far more difficult, the fine for being discovered fornicating in one's chamber at the Inn was five times as great.

After looking at the gates, turn left and go back a few yards to the first staircase entrance which faces the garden of New Square; it is marked no. 12. At the entrance are the names of the barristers who work here. Practicing barristers come mostly from the English upper classes, and the names on these staircases give some interesting insights into the naming habits of grand English people. At no. 12 you may see names with three initials, often a mark of pride in ancestry, suggesting that one has several forebears who deserve commemorating. You may also find a compound surname on this staircase; these are called "double-barrelled" names in England, and are virtually unknown among the working class. They often originated with a marriage between two propertied families, or when a grand person became dissatisfied with being plain Smith or Jones. It is also thought rather splendid to have a *de* or *le* before one's surname; it isn't very chic in England to *be* French, but it is chic to be English with a hint of French ancestry. This feeling goes back to the Middle Ages, when the ruling class in England was of Norman-French descent.

Barristers remain a posh group partly because of the structure of the profession. Young barristers are not allowed simply to set up new practices (called "chambers") of their own; they must join one of the established chambers. And when established barristers decide whom to admit to their chambers, they frequently favor people from their own social background. If a young lawyer succeeds in the fierce competition for a place in chambers, he or she must expect, because of inexperience, to be given little work and to make little or no money for a year or two. The rent and expenses of the chambers, however, are high: the result of beginning one's career in chambers may be no net income at all, or even debt. This arrangement tends to exclude those without family money behind them. Young lawyers without inherited wealth usually become solicitors rather than barristers.

After passing nos. 12 and 13, notice the little grassy courtyard behind railings on the left, and the fine old bow window in the corner. Where the railings end, turn left into the alley; a few yards along, look up and you'll see—about 8 feet above you—an inscription on the wall from 1693, a time when not all of this area belonged to Lincoln's Inn: "This wall is built upon the ground of Lincolnes Inne. No windowes are to be brocken out without leave." Go a little farther down the alley; on the right is an amusing result of local social divisions—a set of segregated washrooms. The notices above the different entrances are, "Members and

tenants only," "Only for clerks employed in Lincoln's Inn," and most exclusive of all, "Benchers only."

Go back down the alley into New Square, and turn left. On staircase no. 1, you will see the name of a firm of solicitors. Over most of England and Wales solicitors are far more numerous than barristers, and their job seems to the public rather less exciting. Much of their work, such as drawing up wills and arranging the sale of real estate, doesn't involve action in the courts. In the relatively humble magistrates' and county courts a solicitor may act in place of a barrister, speaking and cross-questioning on behalf of a client. Some solicitors would like the right to do this in the higher courts as well; barristers, however, defend their near-monopoly by saying that solicitors are not trained in pleading and interrogation, or in the rather stagey techniques by which a barrister sometimes impresses a jury.

Right ahead of you, between staircases 3 and 4, is an arched passage leading out of New Square. On either side of the passage (officially, Lincoln's Inn Archway, Carey Street, London WC2) is Wildy's, established here in 1830, one of the best secondhand legal bookshops in the country. The staff is kind and knowledgeable.

In the windows on the right of the passage Wildy's keeps permanently on show two colorful cartoons which pleasantly satirize the legal industry. One is by H. M. Bateman, an artist who specialized in depicting social blunders—like someone in a concert audience clapping between the movements of a symphony. The cartoon here is called "The Spoilsport," or "The culprit who admitted everything," and shows a cheerful defendant ending his trial on its opening day by telling a horrified court that he is guilty. The judge tries to silence him, while rows of lawyers stare aghast at the prospect of losing a long and juicy case. The other cartoon shows two farmers in a dispute over a cow. One pulls its tail and the other its horns. Between them sits a barrister, in wig and gown, milking it. I asked at Wildy's whether the people who buy these cartoons are lawyers, and was told "Oh yes, nearly always—especially American lawyers. English lawyers perhaps find them rather near the bone."

Barristers, Carey Street

Contrary to popular belief, barristers' earnings are often low by professional standards. There are between three and four thousand practicing barristers in England and Wales (Scotland has its own legal system); in 1977 their organization, the Bar Council, complained that at least a third were earning "a pittance." An English barrister would be lucky, after taking a university degree and having five years' legal practice, to earn as much as an intelligent secretary with no legal qualifications working for the U.S. Supreme Court. English fees can be so low that even the barristers' austere set of rules sometimes relents. Very occasionally a defendant finds himself unrepresented in court, and is allowed to choose any barrister present to represent him. The fee for this work, called "dock defence," is token. Most barristers eagerly avoid it, and evasive measures are permitted. As a legal textbook puts it, "There is no objection to a barrister leaving the court on hearing the prisoner ask for a dock defence, but he should not remove his wig and remain in court." Snatching off one's wig is not allowed, but running for the door is fine.

At the far end of Wildy's passage, look up at the large gaslight, which still functions. Go a few steps towards the road, then look back; in the lawyers' windows above the passage you can often see bundles of papers tied up with legal red tape (literally).

Turn right on leaving the passage, into Carey Street. "To be in Carey Street" is a phrase in England meaning "to be bankrupt." The grand set of buildings facing you, opened in 1882, is called the Law Courts (officially, The Royal Courts of Justice), the main group of civil courts in the country. The bankruptcy court is part of this complex. More about the Law Courts in a moment. First, though, have a look at the lawyers' pub, The Seven Stars, 50 yards along Carey Street on the right. Best viewed from the far side of the road, the building has been here since (it's claimed) 1602. Its two-storied frontage leans out slightly into the street, looking tiny against the backs of the Lincoln's Inn buildings that rise behind it. On the wall of the second story is a metal fire mark, prettily painted, from around 1800. It shows clasped hands, and was put up by an

The Law Courts

Making a full-bottomed wig

insurance company called the Amicable Contributors.

Inside the pub are some large and prized antique mirrors, advertising forgotten brews of beer. The low ceilings bulge slightly. On the walls are old prints of noted lawyers, and of characters from the novels of Dickens. The staff I met seemed frightened to talk about the place. The brewers who own most of Britain's pubs like to install managers without security of tenure. Tenants (who do have security) and owner-managers usually have more confidence and more pride in the places they run. It is sad when the management of a fine pub like this feels that all questions about it have to be referred to the public relations department of a large brewing corporation.

The Law Courts here are built in a lofty Victorian Gothic style, with pinnacles and pointed windows, and faced in stone with bands of red brick. The stone corridors inside seem designed to resemble a medieval castle; and when I walked through them during a rainstorm they were leaking like one. For much of the year the court buildings are closed or almost empty, so I haven't routed the walk through them. If you do go in, you will find an entrance 20 yards beyond The Seven Stars. Remember that these are mainly civil courts. The Old Bailey, the Central Criminal Court, is about a half mile away to the east; that's the place for watching the big names of the criminal world—hit men, domestic murderers and disgraced politicians. Many of the cases here are commercial. When occupied, each courtroom has a list of its cases posted outside. If you plan to stay for a good while, sit in almost any courtroom; otherwise, peep in through the glass in the court's antechamber. Even if they see you, the judges will pretend not to notice. And you do have a right to be there.

In the corridors you may see barristers talking with their clients. There's some discreet drama going on here. The barristers often look very tall with their long gowns and their upright bearing. As a barrister tilts his head back slightly, to look down at a client, the unspoken message is that the client is really rather lucky to be represented by such a grand person. Stagey behavior isn't restricted to the courtroom.

Back in Carey Street, retrace your route, and after passing Wildy's entrance you will see a fine house (no.

60) with wooden shutters on the first story and a fan-light above the door. Immediately after this house turn left into Star Yard. Twenty yards up here, on the right, is the legal wig-making department of the firm Ede and Ravenscroft. A barrister's wig is displayed in the window. The wigs are expensive; the small wig with pigtails used by barristers costs well over £100. (The same design is used for men and women.) The long full-bottomed wigs used by judges on ceremonial occasions cost almost four times as much and take over two years to make. All the wigs are made of South American horsehair, and are meant to last a lifetime. Because of the cost of purchase, judges and barristers commonly borrow wigs from one another.

The wearing of legal wigs has lasted from the seventeenth century; law is a conservative profession dominated by the elderly. It is sometimes argued that the uniform of wig and gown distracts attention from the individuality of the lawyer, helping him or her to appear almost as a personification of the law. The uniform may also persuade the public that barristers are rather majestic people, and that a client is getting good value!

Thirty yards farther up Star Yard is a rare sight in England, a tiny street urinal, made of decorative ironwork. It stands against a back wall of Lincoln's Inn. It's for men only. Notice the royal coats of arms on it, and the iron latticework at the top.

Go back down Star Yard, cross Carey Street, and walk down the pathway that faces you called Bell Yard. At the far end of this path, almost 200 yards away, is a main road—the junction of The Strand (to the right) and Fleet Street (to the left). The traffic makes this spot too noisy to enjoy for long, but notice, before you go, the complicated monument on the right in the middle of the road. Positioned here in 1880, it has a dragon on top and statues of royalty lower down. The site is called Temple Bar, and has been for centuries a point of entry into the City of London from Westminster; barriers of various kinds have stood here since the Middle Ages. (As you stand at the bottom of Bell Yard, the City lies to your left, and West-

Miniature sculpture of Queen Victoria,
Temple Bar

minster to the right.) When a sovereign enters the City from Westminster on a ceremonial occasion, the Lord Mayor of London presents him or her, at Temple Bar, with a sword representing the armed might of the City. The sovereign then gives it back, as if to say, "You use it to look after me." Cross the main road, and from the far side you will see a miniature representation of this scene, sculpted on the side of the monument; Queen Victoria is shown in a carriage, entering the City at the start of her reign in 1837. On horseback and drawing his sword, the Lord Mayor comes to meet her. This ceremony, which occurred again in 1977 at the Jubilee of Elizabeth II, was first recorded in the late sixteenth century. Probably the ceremony goes back to the time when the City was almost an independent little state within England, and the sovereign genuinely had to ask permission to enter.

Until the eighteenth century, this busy place was used for displaying the heads of people executed for treason. The heads had to be fastened high up, so that sympathizers could not easily rescue and bury them. But this meant that some people had difficulty making out the features of the dead men's faces. To meet this important need, traders operated here with telescopes. In August 1746 a literary gent named Horace Walpole wrote in a letter, "I have this morning passed under the new heads at Temple Bar, where people make a trade of letting spying-glasses at a halfpenny a look."

A few yards away at no. 3 Fleet Street is an excellent and old-fashioned tobacconist, Weingott's. Here since 1859, the shop is furnished in nineteenth-century mahogany. Notice also the long wooden counter—a rare survivor. The shop is one of the last in the country to sell loose tobacco, weighed by hand, in large quantities. There are brass scales on the counter, and rows of earthenware jars behind. Lawyers from the Temple are among the main customers. I was told of one well-known judge who in recent years has bought his snuff here, blended to his own specifications. Visitors especially favor the large London-made briar pipes and Havana cigars. The wry and friendly assistant who told me about the shop (he asked to be called just "Cyril") has worked in Fleet Street for over forty years. The square mile or so of the old City, with its hidden alleyways and courtyards, its long-established firms and

Wig & Pen Club, Temple Bar

rather polite working people, creates a loyalty and pride in many of those who know it well. Cyril told me that he thought it "the finest place to work in the world."

A few yards farther into the City, on the right, you will pass the grand seventeenth-century entrance to the Middle Temple. (To see it properly you may want to cross the street again for a moment.) It's built in stone and red brick with pilasters; the Latin inscription means "This went up at the expense of the Middle Temple Society, 1684." Forty yards farther along the street, again on the right, is an even older entrance to the Temple, which we shall go through in a few minutes. First, have a look at the partly timbered building above the entrance, no. 17; it's unusual in several ways. It's one of the very few domestic buildings in London to have survived from Shakespeare's day— most of the City of London was destroyed by the Great Fire of 1666, which stopped just a few yards from here. Permission to build this house was given in 1610; you will notice that it overhangs the street slightly—the builder asked to "jettie out" by twenty-eight inches in addition to the window. Until the late eighteenth century, houses were usually not numbered, but many had names and signs instead, like pubs today. Traces of these old house signs have now almost entirely disappeared; for one thing, in the nineteenth century respectable people didn't want their homes mistaken for pubs! But this building is a rare exception. In the seventeenth century it was named The Prince's Arms, after Prince Henry, the short-lived son of James I. Carved in the woodwork at the front of the house you can see the three feathers, the traditional badge of the Prince of Wales, the heir apparent. In the seventeenth century the building became a tavern for a while, and in 1665, during the Great Plague (which killed about a quarter of London's population), "remedies" for the disease were sold here.

On afternoons during the week, this old house is open to the public. Go up the stairs at the left of the frontage and you will come into a large room overlooking Fleet Street. Wooden paneling and an elaborate plaster ceiling survive from the seventeenth century; and in the middle of the ceiling is another reference to Prince Henry. Although this room has no special connection with Samuel Pepys, it has been interestingly equipped as a memorial to him. On the wall hangs a page from a seventeenth-century satire that attacked Pepys and his clerk, Will Hewer, for the bribes they took at the Navy Office—it mentions gifts of wine, chocolate, anchovies and oysters.

When you are back in Fleet Street, go through the passage underneath the house, past the newspaper vendors who have a thriving business on weekdays. Once through the passage, you will notice that the noise of Fleet Street falls away, and you are in the Temple.

"The Temple" is not the name of a building, but means rather the large site which was once the English headquarters of the Templar knights and is now occupied by two adamantly independent Inns of Court. The sites of the Inner Temple and Middle Temple interlock slightly, as you will see, but the Inner Temple has most of its buildings to the east (left) of the lane where you now are, while most of the Middle Temple is to the west. Thirty yards down this lane, stop and look at the first staircase on the right. Among the barristers' names you may see that of Mr. John Mortimer, a well-known English liberal and defense lawyer, who is also a successful TV playwright. In the late 1970s, Mr. Mortimer created a popular series about an amiable defense barrister, not entirely unlike himself, called "Rumpole of the Bailey."

Like many other barristers named on these staircases, Mr. Mortimer is a Queen's Counsel (nearly always called simply "Q.C."—one of the senior grade of barristers appointed by government committee). In newspaper reports of a Q.C.'s legal work the highly prized initials appear after his or her name. But you won't see them on the staircase boards; for one thing, the rules against advertising by barristers are very strict. Also, a modern tradition against boasting may be at work here; boasting is meant to be done subtly or not at all. A surgeon, for example, who approaches the top of the profession in England and becomes a hospital consultant, ceases to be called "Dr." and becomes plain "Mr." or "Mrs." University teachers at Oxford and Cambridge similarly refuse at times to use the

THIRD FLOOR

Mr & Mrs
John BURRELL
(Entrance at N°2 →
← Third Sir Francis & Lady
Floor PURCHAS

Second Floor

Mr. David WIDDICOMBE

Enquiries please to Clerks Room
2 Mitre Court →
2nd Floor

First Floor

MARRIS
~ & ~
# SHEPHERD

SOLICITORS
Commissioners for Oaths

J.R.H. LANDER
G.R. WHEELER

Please apply N°2 ☜

Ground Floor
Lord HODSON
Lord SIMON of Glaisdale
Sir Trevor REEVE
Dame Margaret BOOTH
Dame E. BUTLER-SLOSS
Mr. Joseph JACKSON
Mr. J.C.J. TATHAM
Mr. Mathew THORPE
Mr. Paul FOCKE
Mr. Peter SINGER
Miss Mary HOGG
Mr. Michael HOROWI
Mr. Nicholas WALL
Mr. Bruce BLAIR
Mr. Richard BON
Miss Judith HUGH
Mr. Martin POINT
Mr. Valentine Le GR

Clerk: Richard

Judge M.V. ARGYLE: Judge Arth
Judge Richard VICK
Judge COPPLESTONE-BOUGHE
Mr. C.R. BEDDINGTON: Mr. Basil GAR

N°.
1

title "Dr." This may be a discreet way of boasting that one no longer needs to boast!

Beside the staircase entrances on this block are badges showing the symbol of the Inner Temple: Pegasus, the winged horse. There is a theory that this badge developed from the seal of the Templar knights. The Templars, being monks and sworn to poverty, liked to advertise their economical ways; their seal showed two knights riding a single horse. When the seal was copied by some later artist, the theory goes, the horse remained but the knights were replaced—perhaps through misunderstanding—by two wings.

When you are level with the second doorway (no. 2) of the block, turn left and walk 40 yards to the gate that is overgrown with creeper (a climbing, ivylike plant). On the way you'll see (to the left) Goldsmith Building, which belongs to the Middle Temple; above its doorway is a stone version of the Inn's badge: the lamb (symbol of Christ) bearing a flag with the sign of the cross. There will be a lot more lambs and flags (and winged horses) along the way; the authorities of the two Inns are very keen to mark their property. (One lawyer complained recently that the badges were even to be found in lavatories.) The lamb and flag here is protected by mesh from birds, but at the time of this writing the birds are winning. Outside Goldsmith Building are two fine, globular gas lamps. If you look on the board at the entrance, the names of the occupants of the third floor may show you that some rooms in the Inns (and especially those on the top stories) are still residential.

When you reach the overgrown gate, turn left and look at two graves—in very different styles. One, from 1726, is of a lawyer named John Hiccocks. Above his tomb is a large stone effigy of the man, gracefully lounging in his finery: long wig, flared coat, breeches and bands (strips of cloth at the neck, still worn by barristers). You can't help contrasting this self-advertisement with the real state of the body underneath. In spite of the boastful grave, Hiccocks is almost entirely forgotten.

Lawyer's chambers, the Temple

The other grave, just to the right, is simple and more often visited; it belongs to Oliver Goldsmith, one of the best-known writers of the eighteenth century. An Irishman, Goldsmith had lodgings in the Temple, and struggled to pay his debts by producing plays and verse. His comedy *She Stoops to Conquer* is still performed in England; it's about a man who mistakes a house for a pub, and treats the worthy occupants of the house as servants. The play is a frequent choice for the dramatic productions of older schoolchildren; there are low-cut dresses and sexual innuendos to keep the kids happy, while Goldsmith's language is old-fashioned enough for the parents to believe the children don't know what's going on.

Goldsmith also wrote a well-known serious poem called "The Deserted Village," the story of a thriving community driven out by a landlord eager to convert his estate to profitable grazing. Goldsmith makes a sentimental but effective contrast between the happy village and the desolate pasture that replaces it. Once there was

The never-failing brook, the busy mill,
The decent church that topt the neighbouring hill,
The hawthorn bush, with seats beneath the shade,
For talking age and whisp'ring lovers made.

But after the landlord has made his changes, there is solitude and emigration:

No more thy glassy brook reflects the day,
But, choked with sedges, works its weedy way . . .
Sunk are thy bowers in shapeless ruin all,
And the long grass o'ertops the mouldering wall;
And, trembling, shrinking from the spoiler's hand,
Far, far away, thy children leave the land.

Goldsmith was buried very close to here, in 1774; the exact site in the churchyard isn't known.

Go back past Goldsmith Building, and look at the Temple Church on the left. This is the only surviving building from the headquarters of the Templar knights. The oldest section of the church is round, modeled on the church of the Holy Sepulchre in Jeru-

Memorial to John Hiccocks, eighteenth-century
lawyer, the Temple

salem; the Templars also got their name from Jerusa-
lem, where they had a base on the site of the old
Temple of Solomon.

The sworn aim of the Templars was to protect the
Holy Land in the Christian interest. This meant fighting
off Muslims—at which the Templars became famously
efficient. Their battle cry, in Latin, had a fine, throb-
bing "no, no, no" sound: *Non nobis, Domine, non
nobis, sed Tuo Nomini da gloriam.* ("Not to us, O
Lord, not to us, but to Thy Name give the glory.")
Even good Islamic warriors must have had doubts
about facing a chanting army of these heavily armed
and sex-starved monks.

The Templars were founded in 1118 by a Frenchman, and France remained their chief recruiting
ground. Their round church here was consecrated in
1185. The windows are rounded at the top in a Ro-
manesque style brought from Normandy. Turn left to
reach the stone porch of the church; underneath is a
superb, broad Norman doorway with a receding set of
decorated, round arches. The huge hinges on the door
form a pleasant design in metal.

The modern entrance to the Temple Church is a few
yards farther around to the left. If you go in, in a moment, you will see on the floor medieval effigies of
knights who were buried here. Also inside, opposite
the modern door, are two vertical slits high in the
stonework; these were the meager windows of the tiny
penitential cell where disobedient Templars were imprisoned.

But first I suggest going into the passage which runs
to the right just beyond the large stone porch. Here,
at the first staircase on the left, you may see listed a
creditable number of women barristers. These chambers are unusual in having so many; in the late 1970s
fewer than one in twelve barristers were women, and
even Conservative lawyers were complaining that
women were discriminated against in admissions to
chambers. Other less serious complaints were made
about the rules for women barristers' dress. Like men,
the women have to wear wig and gown in court; there
are also to be no bare arms or low necklines. On full-
dress occasions, the rules laid down for women Q.C.s
are complex. In 1971 they were reported in W. W.

Bolton's *Guide to Conduct and Etiquette at the Bar:*

> Coat, made up of black superfine cloth; the same style as a man's coat except that it should not be skirted but instead be short as in a lady's ordinary suit—black flexible buttons—plain white blouse—lace "frill" and ruffles at wrist—plain black skirt of superfine cloth—black silk stockings—black patent leather ladies' court shoes—cut steel buckles—black silk gown—full-bottomed wig—black silk "wig bag"—white gloves.

As uniforms go, rather flattering and luxurious—though notice the full-length wig!

A few yards farther on, the passage enters Hare Court. Here, on the far side, were once the chambers of the most notorious of English lawyers, George Jeffreys, the hanging judge of 1685. Jeffreys made his name as an agent of Charles II and of his brother James II. When the Catholic James became King in 1685 numerous Protestants objected, and some backed a rival claimant to the throne—the Duke of Monmouth, an illegitimate son of the late King Charles. (Charles had so many bastards that they were known collectively as "the fraternity.") Monmouth's army was crushed at Sedgemoor in southwestern England, and Jeffreys was then sent, with colleagues, to judge the captives on behalf of King James. The trials of these rebels were hurried, and confessions were improperly extorted. It seems that about 250 were executed on the judge's orders, and there was much disemboweling and quartering. By bullying a witness Jeffreys managed to get an old lady of about seventy condemned for sheltering a rebel. She was beheaded; it was said afterwards that "she was old and dozy and died without much concern." Luckier rebels were transported on Jeffreys's orders to the West Indies, Carolina and Virginia. Samuel Pepys wondered how they were to be treated: "whether to be sold entirely, as blacks are to slavery, for their whole lives, or for how long? . . ." Three years later James II fell. His protégé Jeffreys was imprisoned by the new regime, amid great popular rejoicing, and died in the Tower of London. Lawyers today note that Jeffreys was a talented advocate, and made some unusually precise legal distinctions. Historians point out that there were other, similar, legal murderers—notably in the sixteenth century—who have had much less publicity.

Go back through the passage to the Temple Church. Keep its modern entrance on your left, then walk the length of the courtyard facing you, and through the short tunnel at the end. Once through the tunnel you'll see, about 70 yards ahead, a long line of brick buildings stretching away to the right. This is King's Bench Walk, the most easterly part of the Temple, and worth a close look. The previous buildings on this site were destroyed by the Great Fire of London, and some of the present ones were put up shortly afterwards. Go across to no. 4 and behind its gas lamp you will see the date 1678.

The Great Fire began in early September 1666 on the other side of the City, not far from Tower Hill, and was blown in this direction by a strong east wind. In the previous year there had been another disaster, the plague, and some people thought that this double catastrophe for London was too much of a coincidence—the city was being punished by Heaven. Early in 1666, before the fire, a prophet had foretold religious horrors, after noticing that 666 was the number of the evil beast described in Chapter 13 of the Book of Revelation. When the fire duly came, Puritans seem to have identified the cause of heavenly anger as King Charles, with his relaxed morals and his Catholic brother, James (then known as the Duke of York). So, to appease the public, James arranged to be seen busily fighting the fire. He came to this part of the Temple and sensibly ordered the use of gunpowder on some of the buildings to create a firebreak. At this point a lawyer appeared and "seeing gunpowder brought, came to the Duke and told him it was against the rules and charter of the Temple that anyone should blow that house with gunpowder." But this was no time for due process of law: "Mr. Germaine, the Duke's Master of the Horse, took a cudgel and beat the young lawyer."

Here in the Temple the Great Fire stopped, partly because of the broad, open space but mainly because the east wind died down. Royalists then used the fact in a religious argument of their own. On the great monument to the fire, erected in the 1670s near London Bridge and still standing, it was written that "the fatal fire stopped, as if ordered by Heaven." God wasn't against King Charles after all.

At no. 5 King's Bench Walk were the chambers of one of the Inner Temple's best-known lawyers, Lord Chief Justice Mansfield. (We saw one of Mansfield's residences in Lincoln's Inn Fields.) When an eighteenth-century slave owner brought a slave to England and then tried to take him away again by force, it was Mansfield who ruled in 1772 that this was illegal. This judgment was soon afterwards used as a basis for making all slavery in England illegal. In the 1770s Mansfield was associated with a new law which liberalized the treatment of Roman Catholics, and this drew on him the fury of Protestant crowds. Catholicism was thought to mean tyranny—the behavior of Louis XVI of France was encouraging this view at the time—and in 1780 anti-Catholic crowds raged through London for days, led by a young aristocrat, Lord George Gordon. Mansfield's fine house in Bloomsbury was burned by the rioters; he and his wife narrowly managed to escape out the back.

Go 70 yards down King's Bench Walk, to staircase no. 9. In 1888 this contained the chambers of a certain Montague Druitt, a young barrister who seems never to have been given a case. At the end of that year Druitt drowned himself in the Thames. The authorities of the Inner Temple are not likely to give him much publicity; at present he is the leading suspect for identification as Jack the Ripper.

There were probably five Ripper murders, all in the rough East End of London (little more than a mile from here) during the autumn of 1888. The victims were impoverished prostitutes; the Ripper got his name from the indescribable carvings done to their bodies. The killer was never arrested (so far as is publicly known), but a few months after the last murder a policeman in the East End is said to have told a local vigilante that there would be no more such killings and that the murderer had died in the Thames. The private papers of a London police chief of the period suggest that Druitt was the chief suspect. And there is some evidence that there was once a pamphlet written by a Dr. Lionel Druitt, cousin of Montague, and entitled "The East End Murderer—I Knew Him." At the time of the killings it was suspected that the murderer was a man of genteel appearance, able to win the confidence of his later victims because they were on the lookout for a rough "Ripper type." A very poor man might not have been able to find the privacy to wash the bloodstains from himself and his clothes; a man with money could have had a room of his own nearby—perhaps even on this staircase.

Very like Druitt in appearance, with a similar aquiline nose, was the most interesting of his fellow suspects: Prince Albert Victor, grandson of Queen Victoria and elder son of Edward, Prince of Wales (later Edward VII). Had he lived, Albert Victor would have come to the throne on Edward's death in 1910, but he died young, in 1892, after acquiring a strange reputation. Evidence that he was Jack the Ripper was first claimed publicly in 1970, by an eminent, elderly surgeon named Thomas Stowell. Stowell said that his source for the theory was the private papers of Sir William Gull, physician to the Royal Family in the 1880s. Stowell is now dead, and Gull's papers have never been published. A famous government pathologist said fairly recently that he himself disbelieved Stowell's theory, but that it had been put to him before Stowell published it by "one of the really great authorities on Jack the Ripper." Buckingham Palace, understandably, has denied the charge that Jack the Ripper might have been the Queen's great-uncle.

Albert Victor, like Druitt, was connected with the Temple; in 1885 he was elected an honorary member of the Middle Temple's governing body. Whether or not either of these men was the Ripper, the Temple was certainly a wild place in the nineteenth century. The residents, many of them not lawyers, were virtually uncontrolled. One prostitute reported that her colleagues were afraid to go there, and that a shrewd woman would prefer to jump from a moving cab rather than be taken by a man to the Temple.

Go back up King's Bench Walk for 40 yards, then turn left and cross the wide parking lot to enter the lane directly opposite. The first block on the left is called the Paper Buildings; at its entrance (staircase 1) notice the splendidly Dickensian name of a solicitors' firm, Griffinhoofe and Co. Beyond the Paper Buildings, on the left, are the gardens of the Inner Temple (unfortunately, closed to the public). It was here that Shakespeare imagined the symbolic beginning of the Wars of the Roses, the long fifteenth-century civil wars between the dynastic houses of Lancaster and York. Lancaster was symbolized by the red rose, York by the white. In *Henry VI* Shakespeare describes a quarrel in the Temple garden between the Yorkist character Richard Plantagenet and the Lancastrian Earl of Somerset, in which the emblems were chosen.

PLANTAGENET: Let him that is a true-born gentleman . . .
　　　　　　　From off this brier pluck a white rose with
　　　　　　　me.
　SOMERSET: Let him that is no coward nor no flatterer . . .
　　　　　　　Pluck a red rose from off this thorn with
　　　　　　　me . . .
PLANTAGENET: Hath not thy rose a canker, Somerset?
　SOMERSET: Hath not thy rose a thorn, Plantagenet?
PLANTAGENET: . . . . by my soul, this pale and angry rose,
　　　　　　　As cognizance of my blood-drinking hate,
　　　　　　　Will I for ever, and my faction, wear,
　　　　　　　Until it wither with me to my grave,
　　　　　　　Or flourish to the height of my degree.

These gardens were extended in the 1860s, when the making of the Thames Embankment narrowed the river and created new land. At the time there was an official plan to build docks on the river frontage, but the lawyers of the Temple were appalled at this threat to their peace, and no doubt applied pressure in high places. A compromise was reached about the new land: no docks, but no large buildings for the lawyers either. So they enlarged their gardens instead.

Pass the elaborate iron gates dated 1730 which lead to the gardens. (Just through the gates you'll see a fine bed of red and white roses in summer.) Continue along the lane until the gardens end; just beyond this point is a stone arch, and on the other side runs Middle Temple Lane to the left and right. Turn left into the lane for a moment, and look at the stone buildings which arch across it farther down. These were put up in the 1870s, jointly by the Inner Temple (to the left of the Lane) and the Middle Temple (to the right). The scheme made for increased quarreling between the two bodies. The Inner Temple wanted to build in stone, to match its existing structures; the Middle Temple wanted brick for the same reason. On this point the Inner Temple won. But then came a juicier legal issue: who owned that section of the new building which was directly over the lane? The Inner Temple claimed a share in it, because architecturally it could hardly exist without the adjoining section which is on Inner Temple land. But the Middle Temple argued that because the soil of Middle Temple Lane was *its* property, the building over the lane must also be. Being experienced lawyers, the gentlemen of the two Inns preferred not to settle the issue in court. The Middle Temple took two of the four floors, and allowed the Inner Temple to have a lease of the other two for 999 years at a yearly rent of two shillings (a tenth of a pound).

Come back up Middle Temple Lane and turn into the first courtyard that appears on your left, Fountain Court. The building on your left as you enter the court is the hall of the Middle Temple; it was built in the 1560s and 1570s, during the reign of Elizabeth I. The exterior of the hall was renovated in the eighteenth century, but the interior remains largely as it was in Tudor times. On the roof of the hall is a pretty cupola (also called a lantern); the present one is not the original, but there has been a cupola in this position since the 1570s. Its original use wasn't merely decorative; it had to let out smoke without letting in rain. The fireplace of the hall was in mid-floor; there was no chimney for it—the smoke just wandered upward and drifted out of the cupola.

The Elizabethan naval warrior, Sir Francis Drake, once staged a grand theatrical entry here. In August 1586, Drake had just returned from a successful expedition (plundering Spanish possessions) and, while the lawyers were dining in the hall, he unexpectedly swept in. He was a member of the Middle Temple, and the records of the Inn (kept in bad Latin) say that he was received with great rejoicing. A few years earlier, Drake and his men had become the first Englishmen to sail round the world; during the voyage they had landed in California and rather optimistically claimed the place for Queen Elizabeth.

In February 1602, almost at the end of the Queen's long reign, there was some real theater here in the hall. A Middle Temple barrister noted in his diary, "February 2nd. At our feast we had a play called *Twelfth Night,* or *What You Will,* much like *The Comedy of Errors . . .*" This is the first recorded performance of Shakespeare's play. Unfortunately, the barrister doesn't mention who the actors were, but it was twenty years before the play was published in print, and it is argued that only Shakespeare's company is likely to have acted from the manuscript version. If so, Shakespeare himself was probably among the actors.

Later in the seventeenth century there were wild disturbances in the hall. The students and young barristers of the Middle Temple used to hold "Grand Christmasses," with much drinking and gambling. (In the eighteenth century, when part of the interior of the hall was renovated, about a hundred ancient dice were discovered, which had been lost in the original floor.) The Grand Christmas of 1629 was especially lively; the authorities of the Inn canceled the celebration for the following year. But the young gentlemen disobeyed, entered the hall and, when the steward refused to bring them food, locked him in the stocks. The authorities retaliated with punishments, at which the students here approached the Benchers in hall to protest. On being turned away, they "hasted down tumultuously, and calling for pots threw them at random toward the Bench table and struck several masters."

In November 1639 the hall was locked to prevent another Grand Christmas. But various members of the Inn "with their swords drawne in a contemptuous and riotous manner assembled themselves and did by violences breake open the dores of the hall, butterie and kitchin and did sett up commons [food] and playe [gambling]." Today's younger barristers and legal students act in striking contrast to their spirited seventeenth-century predecessors. Anxious to be accepted into chambers, or relieved to be there, they are controlled far more by the fear of their elders' disapproval. Unnaturally sedate behavior is the norm, and some young lawyers attempt to look middle-aged prematurely, so as not to put off clients by seeming young and inexperienced.

The hall of the Middle Temple is open from Monday through Saturday, morning and afternoon (between 12:00 noon and 3:00 it's normally shut for lunch). If you go in, you will notice that around the windows are weapons and pieces of armor, most of them from Elizabethan times. Below the third window on the south side (the long side away from the entrance) is a bulging "globose" breastplate from the reign of Elizabeth's father, Henry VIII. The most famous feature of the hall is the interior of its roof: it is supported by a double bank of Elizabethan hammer beams (beams which stand out only a short way from the walls and do not span the width of the hall). Behind the high table are large portraits of monarchs, including seventeenth-century paintings of Charles II and his brother James II. As you leave the hall, look at the intricately carved wooden screen with its double door; it was made to restrict access to the hall after another disorderly Grand Christmas in 1670. Above it, in a fleur-de-lis design, are iron spikes to prevent young lawyers from swarming over the top.

Outside the hall, under the trees in the courtyard, is a fountain; there has been one here since 1681. Dickens was fond of the place; for him it was a symbol of life amid legal sterility. In *Martin Chuzzlewit* he says:

> Brilliantly the Temple fountain sparkled in the sun, as little Ruth and her companion came towards it. There Tom could see her . . . coming briskly up, with the best little laugh upon her face that ever played in opposition to the fountain. The fountain might have leapt up twenty feet to greet this spring of hopeful maidenhood that in her person stole through the dry and dusty channels of the law. . . .

Psychologists might have something to say about the symbolism here—the springs of maidenhood and leaping (male) fountains; Dickens, as is well known, had an intense imagination!

To the right, in the far corner of Fountain Court just behind the trees, is a gate leading to a pub, the Devereux. On summer mornings the path between the pub and the court is often taken over by well-dressed, youngish legal men with pint glasses in hand. Through the crowd step barristers in twos and threes on their way from the law courts, wigs and gowns removed but white bands still in place at the neck. At the Devereux the strong beer (Director's) is good; this is also a reasonable place for a pub lunch. Better still is The George, 50 yards along the passage, to the right.

Perhaps the best place to end this walk is back in Fountain Court. There are seats by the fountain itself, and also a view into the Middle Temple gardens by the end of the hall. Lawyers have occupied the Temple since the fourteenth century. The story of how they came to replace the Templar knights involves one of the greatest crimes of the Middle Ages, and makes a tragic epilogue to the walk.

In 1291 the Templars lost their most respected function—guarding the Holy Land. Acre, the last Christian toehold in Palestine, had fallen to the Muslims. Over the years the Templar order had become very rich, with many thousands of landed estates in western Europe. Because they were wealthy and involved in banking, the knights had made enemies, and after the fall of Acre some of these opponents saw their chance. Chief among them was Philippe IV (Philip the Handsome) of France.

Philippe tried to unite the two main orders of fighting monks, the Templars and the Knights of St. John ("The Hospitallers"), hoping to become the ruler of the large new organization and to gain control of Templar wealth. But the chief of the Templars, a distinguished warrior named Jacques de Molay, opposed this, and Philippe retaliated by organizing a coup. What happened was that on October 12, 1307, de Molay was an honored participant alongside the King at a royal funeral. Early the next morning, Templars were arrested all over France on orders from Philippe issued secretly long before. Shocking confessions then began to emerge; Templars stated that they had denied Christ, spat on the crucifix, taken homosexual vows and worshipped the devil. Jacques de Molay himself confessed. Philippe now had a case for seizing the vast Templar wealth, which he did.

But were the confessions true? Some Templar knights who had been captured by Muslims chose to spend years in the jails of Syria and Egypt rather than deny Christ. In confessions about devil worship, it was stated that the devil had taken the form of a black cat, which had afterwards disappeared miraculously into a wall. During examination, one Templar revealed the main reason for these strange confessions—by producing the bones of his own foot, roasted off under torture. The knights, including de Molay, had been savagely tortured by the Church authorities to extract "admissions." The Pope at the time, Clement V, was a Frenchman under Philippe's control; he owed his position to the King. He collaborated vigorously in the persecution. Templars were promised their freedom if they confessed, imprisonment and death if they did not.

In England, the young King Edward II at first stated that the charges against the Templars were incredible, and the English Church authorities tended to agree. But Edward was Philippe's son-in-law, and very much under his influence. Philippe and the Pope pressed hard to get the English Templars tortured; claims about Templar wickedness in France would look very strange if in neighboring England the knights were still to be honored as holy men. Some torture was eventually applied in England and the Master of the Temple here, William de la More, died a prisoner in the Tower of London. In England, as in France, the Templar order was dissolved.

There was a strange sequel. In 1314 Jacques de Molay withdrew his confession, saying that his only great shame was to have confessed falsely in the first place. Philippe responded by having him burned on an island in the Seine. But many French people understandably refused to believe the accusations against the Templars: some of the more enthusiastic collected de Molay's ashes and treated them as the relics of a saint. It came to be said that as de Molay died in the flames he had cursed King Philippe. Later events certainly suggested the working of a curse: Philippe died within a few months; so did Pope Clement; and in England Edward II, who had eventually joined in the persecutions, was horribly murdered with a red-hot poker (driven into an unmentionable part of his body). Later French monarchs who came to a bad end were regarded as "the accursed kings" (*les rois maudits*), still suffering from the curse of the Templars.

In France the treasures of the Templar knights were never recovered from royal hands. In England the

Temple passed during the 1320s into the keeping of the Hospitallers, and they soon let it to the secular lawyers, who have been here ever since. The lawyers of the Temple have, of course, always been largely concerned with the defense of private property. It is ironic that when they first moved to this pleasant and highly valued site it was still very obviously stolen goods— improperly confiscated from the tortured and humiliated monks of war.

The Old Palace Quarter: St. James's

This busy and fashionable district, best visited on a weekday, has narrow streets, famous shops and little-known courtyards. It grew up alongside the Tudor palace of St. James's; its grandest thoroughfare, St. James's Street, runs downhill to the palace gates and is lined with eighteenth-century buildings. Just a few yards away, out of view in dark passages, crime and vice used to flourish; one such alley has survived and will be on this route. Gaslit and crowded with humble shops, it keeps its working-class character just a few yards away from the palace.

The palace itself was built by King Henry VIII in the 1530s, during the time of his second, third and fourth queens. The area then seemed rather remote, away in the fields, several minutes' walk to the west of the palace of Whitehall. For many years St. James's had been used to isolate a colony of leper women. When the King seized the property of Catholic organizations, these women were sent away. Remains of their buildings were found in fairly recent times inside the palace. Several parts of King Henry's structure are still standing; you'll see them towards the end of the walk.

The architecture of the palace is enjoyable but not imposing. Some later monarchs and their subjects became ashamed of St. James's; in the eighteenth century it was criticized by John Fielding (a magistrate, whose brother Henry wrote *Tom Jones*): "The buildings that compose this merely nominal palace (for by all rules of architecture it has no claim to the title) are low, plain, and ignoble, devoid of any exterior beauty. . . . It reflects no honour on the kingdom, and is the jest of foreigners." Many rulers treated St. James's as a reserve palace, Whitehall being the chief one until it was burned in 1698. In the mid-eighteenth century George III was probably rather relieved to move his residence to Buckingham House (later Buckingham Palace), just a few hundred yards away. But some members of the

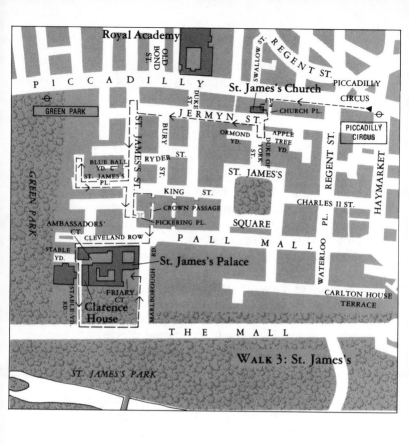

royal family continued to live at St. James's Palace, and ambassadors of foreign states are still called "Ambassadors to the Court of St. James's." Close to the palace you will see an ancient building where ministers of the short-lived Republic of Texas had their legation in the 1840s.

To serve royalty and the numerous courtiers and hangers-on, shops of unusual quality were opened in the area. Some of them are still in business after two centuries or more. Most of the shops in St. James's charge high prices, as they probably always have. But unlike posh shops in other parts of Britain, their atmosphere isn't overpoweringly grand. For one thing, property has long been so expensive here that even stylish businesses have traditionally been squeezed into narrow and homely buildings.

Some of the finest old houses lie in quiet passages off St. James's Street. On the way to them we shall look at this street itself; although loud and busy nowadays, it contains some of the world's oldest and most exclusive gentlemen's clubs. These places have for centuries provided lodging, drink and food for the aristocracy and gentry. Only in the last few years have women been allowed in, whether as members or guests. In the eighteenth century politicians and men of fashion gambled here, sometimes in public view, for almost unimaginably large fortunes. Although housed in impressive buildings, these clubs don't display their names outside; the idea perhaps is that *gentlemen* know where the clubs are, and the others . . . well, why tell them?

From Piccadilly tube station, walk 150 yards down the left side of Piccadilly itself. Turn left into the alley called Church Place. A few yards along here on the right is a gate which leads down steps to a business called The London Brass-Rubbing Centre. This is worth a visit, whether or not you intend to rub brasses. In the large room downstairs brass-rubbing equipment is sold, and people rent—fairly cheaply—facsimiles of medieval and later brasses, which they then rub on the premises. The original brasses are flat effigies of wealthy men and women, wearing the fashions of their day, set up as memorials in English churches. The staff here give advice on how to transfer the designs to paper laid over the effigies—the same principle that children use when scribbling on paper pressed over a coin. They will help you to rectify any mistakes; I was told that even complete beginners usually produce copies they are proud of. The smaller the effigy, the less it costs. (The largest effigy, of a medieval knight in armor, is life-size. Tiny effigies, which are popular with children, are also available.) With enthusiasts around the shop busily creating their own copies of these antique figures, this is perhaps one of London's most pleasant businesses. Rubbings ready-made by professionals can also be bought here. Specialists interested in visiting country churches where original brasses can be rubbed on site should contact Phillips and Page (50 Kensington Church Street, W8). This firm is said to be the mecca of brass-rubbing cognoscenti, and gives practical information such as the telephone numbers of relevant rural vicars.

Go back into Piccadilly and turn left. Ten yards along are the railings of the churchyard of St. James's.

Go in through the gateway to look at the church itself. It was designed by Christopher Wren, the most fashionable architect of the late seventeenth century, and was built between 1676 and 1684. The exterior is plain, too plain for many people's tastes; Wren was under pressure to economize and reserved the elaboration for the interior. The outdoor pulpit next to the church wall was put up in 1902, in the last days of horse-drawn traffic and just before the noise of motors in Piccadilly made it virtually unusable. Before entering, go around to the right of the church tower. On the keystone of the arch you will see a coat of arms showing stars and a crescent moon. This was the badge of Henry Jermyn, Earl of St. Albans, the chief contributor of funds for building the church. Helped by his influence at court, he also took the lead in laying out many of the fine streets of St. James's. He was a friend of Henrietta Maria, widow of the executed King Charles I and mother of the reigning Charles II. It was rumored at court that Charles II wanted Jermyn to join him in a ménage à trois with the royal mistress Barbara Villiers. (More on this rapacious lady later, when we reach the site of her mansion near the palace.) Go up the steps into the garden of the church. From here, under the plane trees, you get an unusual view of the narrow and chic Jermyn Street which runs below. When you are in the street (in a few minutes) you'll probably give most of your attention to the shop fronts. But from here you notice more easily the tall and elegant façades, from the eighteenth and nineteenth centuries, which rise above the shops.

In the late eighteenth century the area near the church became very dangerous at night. In 1774 an extra ten watchmen were hired by the parish, and provided with cutlasses, carbines and wooden noise-makers to raise the alarm. In 1793 still more watchmen were employed, to deal with "the alarming increase of a most daring and desperate set of thieves, who are harbored in and nightly infest this parish." In the dark streets even time-consuming crimes went on in public; in the 1790s a parish committee here was troubled by numerous thefts of iron railings.

Go back to the church tower, and enter by the door

Window, St. James's Church

facing Piccadilly. Just inside, on the left, is a modern plaque in honor of the poet and artist William Blake, who was baptized here in 1757. Blake became highly fashionable in Britain in the late 1960s, when pale and long-haired young men, who looked like radicals but were not, found satisfaction in his white, elongated figures.

Inside the church, with its side galleries and rounded baroque arches, Wren's general design is still clear. Many details were restored after the bombing in 1940. Four thousand books of gold leaf were used to gild the new ceiling. Wren was proud of the original interior; writing about St. James's, he explained why Protestant churches such as this needed to be small: to allow the worshippers to see and hear all the proceedings, and thus to have informed consciences. (An informed conscience, rather than a priest, was thought by Protestants to be the proper link with God.) "The Romanists may build larger churches; it is enough if they hear the murmur of the mass and see the elevation of the host, but ours are to be fitted for auditories."

In spite of Wren's pious purpose, this church was soon being used for unholy social display. One traveler complained in 1722 that renting a seat during a service cost almost the same as a seat at the theater. Nevertheless, the expense was justified "on a holiday or Sunday, when the fine assembly of beauties and quality come there." Earlier, in 1703, the diarist John Evelyn referred to St. James's as one of the "theatrical churches." Thieves were attracted; in 1693 the authorities here paid ten shillings, a large sum, to a man named Simmonds "for his care in looking after and taking pickpockets in the church."

On entering the body of the church, turn left toward the white marble font, where Blake was christened. Around the stem are carved Adam, Eve and the serpent. This is the work of Grinling Gibbons, the master carver of Wren's day. Gibbons also did the very ornate carving in limewood around the altar.

Go along the wall of the church on the side by the font. Beneath the second window is a memorial to one of the last British colonial administrators in Amer-

Outdoor pulpit, St. James's Church

ica, Guy Johnston, "of Guy Park in the Province of New York," who, with typical eighteenth-century nepotism, "succeeded his father-in-law as superintendent of Indian affairs in North America" in 1774. He died fourteen years later—in London.

Just past the fourth window in the same wall is a plaque commemorating a society physician of the early nineteenth century, the baronet Sir Richard Croft. As often happens with pious memorials, the really interesting details aren't recorded. Slim and elegant, Croft was involved, to his cost, in a far-reaching tragedy within the Royal Family. In 1817 Princess Charlotte, only child of George, the Prince Regent, and his estranged wife, Caroline, was due to give birth. Croft was the most noted *accoucheur* of the day, and was appointed to look after her. He put the poor woman on an insubstantial diet and had her bled liberally, to counter what he called her "morbid excess of animal spirits." After being in labor for fifty hours, Charlotte produced a stillborn child. She herself seemed to make a good recovery at first, but after a few hours she relapsed and died for reasons that have never been fully understood. Croft's reputation was ruined. The Prince Regent kindly published a tribute to him, but there was much hostile criticism in the newspapers. A few months later, in February 1818, when attending the confinement of a woman with symptoms similar to Charlotte's, Croft took a pistol from the wall of the patient's house and shot himself. The body of a suicide was not allowed burial in holy ground, and you will notice that the memorial here was put up many years after Croft's death, when the manner of it had ceased to be notorious. In Croft's day, unpopular suicides were still being buried at crossroads, with a stake driven through the heart.

For the Royal Family, the effects of Charlotte's death could hardly have been greater. Had she lived and had descendants, she—and they—would almost certainly have inherited the throne rather than Charlotte's cousin Victoria and her descendants, who have held the throne from 1837 to the present day.

Going back into the vestibule of the church, you will notice a bell rope, with decorative colored grip,

Seventeenth-century font,
St. James's Church

which passes through the ceiling and hangs here. Turn left and you'll come out into Jermyn Street. Across the street, and a few yards to the left, is the start of Duke of York Street; go down this for a moment. The first entry on the left is Apple Tree Yard, now a dull reality with a pretty name. (There will be some fine court-yards later; if you would like to explore one now, op-posite is Ormond Yard, where tiny shops have been created in the backs of the large Jermyn Street build-ings. A gaslight survives around the corner at the far end of Ormond Yard.) On the corner of Apple Tree Yard is Wheeler's, one of a small chain of respected oyster restaurants. They are decorated in a uniform of green paint, with crisscross latticework on the win-dows.

On the opposite side of Duke of York Street, close to Ormond Yard, is perhaps the finest pub in the area, The Red Lion. Look at it first from Wheeler's corner. The present building is mainly from the early nine-teenth century. It is four-storied, with a flat front and rounded garret windows on the top floor. The doors gleam with brass, and even from outside you get a hint of the precious etched glass within. The first story was converted in late Victorian times to form a "gin pal-ace," glittering with glass and mirrors. Historic build-ings such as this are systematically described in the long and authoritative series of volumes called the *Survey of London* now published by the Greater Lon-don Council. Its authors are usually extremely sober in their language, but when they reach The Red Lion ex-citement takes over: "The small interior has a ceiling of cigar-brown lincrusta [embossed oilcloth], the walls and partitions being formed in light arcaded frames of polished mahogany, enclosing glass panels enriched in every possible way[!] with frosted, brilliant-cut and partly mirrored arabesque designs." If you like the old-fashioned English beer, flat and strong, the brew to ask for here is Burton.

Coming back up Duke of York Street, look at the fish shop at no. 1, just before you turn left into Jermyn Street. Behind its large sash window, which is open during business hours, the fish are displayed on a

Fishmonger, Duke of York Street

blue-flecked marble slab. Above the window are fish motifs in art nouveau metalwork.

At the corner with Jermyn Street is a men's clothing shop with pleasantly colored tiles running in bands between its windows. Gents' clothes and shoes are among the expensive specialties of Jermyn Street. Turn left at the corner, and at no. 94 Jermyn Street look in the window of the antiquarian firm of John Faustus. Greek and Roman objects—statuettes, oil lamps, coins—are often on show here. Prices are not displayed. (This is usually a sign that they are high, whether in fashionable St. James's or in a working-class fruit store.) The sources of Faustus's antiques are no doubt entirely proper but many other ancient objects come onto the market by colorful and mysterious means. Among the most important suppliers to the trade are northern Italian tomb-robbers, who probe the ground with long metal rods. (When the rod meets little resistance, that is a sign that an ancient burial chamber may have been reached.) One of Britain's most treasured Greek vases was dug up fairly recently by these characters, who then touted for a buyer by sending bits of it, as samples, to leading museums of the world. (Most of the pieces were eventually bought privately by an acquaintance of mine; he later had to use diplomacy and arm-twisting to extort the remaining pieces from coy museums. The vase was kept at his home, until his children began to use it for storing tennis balls. At this point he decided to offer it, at an artificially low price, to a London museum.)

Next door, at no. 93 (in a building partly of the late seventeenth century), is the firm of Paxton and Whitfield. Notice the brass plates below the window, stretching almost the length of the façade, on which the engraved name of the business has faded with polishing over the years. The firm describes itself, with old-fashioned vagueness, as "provision merchants," but in fact has an international reputation for one thing—cheese. In the window are whole cheeses, especially popular being Blue Stilton, a strong cheese much sought after in the restaurants of Paris, and made only in northeast Leicestershire, a district of the English Midlands. I found the staff very friendly, and

Cheeses and hams, Jermyn Street

customers are allowed to taste before buying. Brass weights are still used on the scale. The sawdust on the floor doesn't mean that the place is rough-and-ready; it's a reminder that the business claims to give excellent old-fashioned service.

Four doors along, at no. 89, is Floris the perfumers, with a discreet window display and a large, bright and coarsely executed royal coat of arms above it, to boast of an exalted patron. Floris has traded here since 1810. Look through the door at the lovely old display cases. The building next door, no. 88, was largely rebuilt about the year 1800, but parts of it remain from the late seventeenth century when it was the home (from 1696 to 1700) of Isaac Newton, one of the greatest of all physicists. It was Newton, for example, who formulated the laws which apply when a vehicle stops abruptly and the driver keeps going. Today it is fashionable among historians to study Newton's less scientific activities. He was a convinced Unitarian, and had to be secretive about this to avoid persecution. He also spent much time carefully examining the accuracy of Old Testament prophecies. In 1700 Newton moved one door down to no. 87, now entirely rebuilt; there is a plaque in his honor.

Across the road at no. 40 is the slightly lurid entrance to an exclusive and much-publicized disco, Tramp. (St. James's is a posh enough district for the name Tramp to be chic and acceptable. In Covent Garden or Soho people might think twice about opening a club with a name like that: they just might get some of the genuine article appearing at the door.)

A few yards farther, on the left of the street, is the jeweler's Grima. Its display windows are small, stylish and irregular—little more than peepholes in the deliberately craggy metal façade. I remember how modern this all looked in 1967, definitely part of Swinging London. Now the building is beginning to look dated and is entering the dangerous period in which good designs are often demolished, when they have ceased to be the latest fashion but are not yet valued as antiques.

On the right of the street is the rear section of Fortnum and Mason's, one of Britain's grandest general stores. Tea at Fortnum's (on the first and fourth sto-

Shopping arcade, Jermyn Street

ries) is a favorite social occasion. The cakes here are especially delicious.

If you're near Fortnum's just before the clocks are due to strike the hours, you may like to turn right here and go for a moment to the front of the building, in Piccadilly. On the third story of the façade is a large ornamental clock. On the hour it chimes delicately; double-leaved miniature doors open on each side of it, and two mechanical figures appear, dressed in the livery of eighteenth-century servants, holding a tray and lighted candles. The tune played by the bells is the song of Eton school. Very touristy, but pretty. Back in Jermyn Street, a few yards farther down on the right, is another reference to Eton. The clothing shop New and Lingwood, at the entrance to Piccadilly Arcade, advertises that it "incorporates W. V. Brown of Eton." Eton is a resonant name in English ears; a small town to the west of London, close to the royal residence of Windsor Castle, Eton contains by far the best-known and most aristocratic of private schools. To have attended Eton often causes one to have one's name mentioned in the gossip columns. Wealthy Englishmen have traditionally defended the privileges of Eton; in the nineteenth century the Duke of Cumberland, one of Queen Victoria's uncles, tried to prevent the building of the Great Western Railway on the grounds that the noise from it would disturb the Eton boys.

A little farther along, Jermyn Street is joined by Bury Street (pronounced "berry"). Bury Street has existed since the late seventeenth century, but its present buildings are relatively new. The freehold of the street is owned by the crown, and the *Survey of London* complains discreetly but persistently about the crown's policy here of demolishing old buildings. In February 1755 there was a dramatic fire in the street, described in a gossipy letter by Horace Walpole:

> I am at present confined with a cold, which I caught by going to a fire in the middle of the night, and in the middle of the snow, two days ago. About 5 in the morning Harry waked me with a candle in his hand, and cried, "Pray, your honour, don't be frightened!" "No, Harry, I am not: but what is it that I am not to be frightened at?" "There is a great fire here in St. James's St." I rose, and indeed thought all St. James's St. was on fire, but it proved in Bury Street. However, you know I can't resist

going to a fire: for it is certainly the only horrid sight that is fine. I slipped on my slippers, and an embroidered suit that hung on the chair, and ran to Bury St., and stepped into a pipe that was broken up for water. It would have made a picture—the horror of the flames, the snow, the day breaking with difficulty through so foul a night, and my figure—mud and gold. There were two houses burnt, and a poor maid; another jumped out of a window and is much hurt, and two young beauties were conveyed out the same way in their shifts.

Seeing young beauties in their nightclothes was one of the rewards of fire gazing, or fire fighting. In the late nineteenth century fire fighting became highly fashionable. The head of the London fire brigade was a glamorous public figure, and the Prince of Wales (later King Edward VII) served as an amateur fireman. One famous advertisement of the time showed a brawny fire fighter descending a rope with a thinly clad beauty fainting over his arm.

At the far left corner of Jermyn Street and Bury Street is a well-known shop for men's shirts, Turnbull and Asser. Over the doorways are prettily painted cherubs. From across the street, look upwards at some imaginative architecture from the early twentieth century. The area above the shop has been designed to resemble an Italian Renaissance tower of seven stories; near the top a miniature colonnade of windows forms an imitation loggia.

A few yards farther, Jermyn Street ends in St. James's Street. Although St. James's Street is noisy and traffic-ridden, some of its buildings are worth a look before you go on to quieter places. Turn to the right for a moment. The eighteenth-century building at no. 37 (two doors up from Jermyn Street) is White's, one of the most famous English clubs for wealthy gentlemen. The club has been on this site since 1755, and began as a chocolate-house in the late seventeenth century, when cocoa was expensive and fashionable. (Supplies of cocoa were said to have been among the bribes offered to Samuel Pepys at the seventeenth-century Navy Office.) Notice the fine lamps at the club door, and the iron boot scrapers.

In the late eighteenth century White's was a club for Tories, the country party of conservatives who supported King George III. The rival, reformist Whigs had their club across the road at Brooks's. (Brooks's is still there, 80 yards down the hill—the building of yellow gray stone with flat pillars built into its frontage. We shall reach it in a moment.) In February 1784 the young Tory Prime Minister, William Pitt, was on his way back from a dinner given in his honor by the Grocers' Company, when he was attacked outside Brooks's by a gang, probably hired by the Whigs. After taking a beating, he narrowly escaped into White's. A Whig poet wrote gleefully:

> See the sad sequel of the Grocers' treat;
> Behold him darting up St. James's Street!
> Pelted and scared by Brooks's hellish sprites,
> And vainly fluttering round the door of White's.

At this period there was extravagant gambling at White's, as at neighboring clubs. (The fashionable term for heavy gambling was "deep play.") A poet made a character say:

> Had I whole counties, I to White's would go,
> And set land, woods and rivers at a throw.

This wasn't a great exaggeration; large landed estates were often lost in an evening's gambling in St. James's Street. Among the favorite games were faro (pronounced "pharaoh") and basset. In both, the players bet on the order in which certain cards would be taken from the top of the deck. In the 1730s the satirical artist William Hogarth portrayed (in a series called "Rake's Progress") a young gambler being arrested for debt in this part of St. James's Street: the gambler steps, shocked, out of his sedan chair to meet the bailiff while a lamplighter, filling an oil lamp nearby, looks on in fascination and spills his oil into the street. As a comment on the feverish gambling of the area, Hogarth also showed small children betting at cards on the sidewalk. In the background to the scene is the Tudor gate house of St. James's Palace. Look down the street and you will see it's still there.

Go back to the corner with Jermyn Street and continue for 60 yards down St. James's Street. At no. 28 (on the left) is perhaps the finest building in the district. It is flanked by two tall wings, like towers, and in the center is a high Venetian window, rising between miniature Ionic columns and surmounted by a

Boodle's, eighteenth-century gambling club, St. James's Street

great fan. This is, and has been since 1783, Boodle's
Club. The building was originally constructed in the
previous decade for another club, the Savoir Vivre,
which had among its members the infamous General
Richard Smith. Smith, a cheese-monger's son from Jermyn Street, had earlier been sent to India, like a lot of
other wild young men whose families weren't alto-
gether appalled by the thought that they might never
come back. But Smith did come back, with a military

title and a fortune. He then tried to set himself up as a Member of Parliament, using bribery so blatantly that even in the corrupt eighteenth century he managed to get sent to prison for it. With his Indian wealth, Smith also became "the deepest of all deep gamesters in London." Horace Walpole describes how Smith and "a set of sharpers" established the Savoir Vivre in this building, forming "a plan for a new club, which, by the excess of play, should draw all the young extravagants thither. They built a magnificent house in St. James's Street, furnished it gorgeously. . . ." Smith and his colleagues were anxious that rich young gamblers should not be restricted in their betting by shortage of ready cash. So, "the titular master of the house the first night acquainted the richest and most wasteful of the members that they might be furnished in the house with loans of ready money, even as far as £40,000." (An ordinary person at that time could live on £50 a year.)

Smith's Savoir Vivre Club was not a success, and after seven years Boodle's took over the premises. This club took its name from Edward Boodle, a genial old scoundrel who had managed it in earlier days (he died in 1772). Boodle had squandered his own large inheritance and enjoyed teaching young men to drink heavily. He made it difficult to escape from his private parties: "when he perceived his young guests begin to flag or become drowsy, he would get up, lock the door of the room and, putting the key in his pocket, strike up the song ' 'Tis not yet day.' "

Look up at the room on the second story, immediately to the left of the grand Venetian window and above the doorway. This is the "Undress Dining-Room"—for dining in informal clothes. Behind the Venetian window itself is the saloon, one-and-a-half stories high.

In the late 1970s, the membership of Boodle's included Mr. John Profumo, once a luckless politician. When Secretary of State for War, he was disgraced in 1963 for having an affair with Christine Keeler, an attractive and very young woman who was also socializing at the time with a Russian agent named Ivanov. The fall of Profumo, all the more spectacular after his public denial of the affair, was a landmark in British social history. Heavy informal censorship and respect for politicians had lingered since the Second World War. In 1963 they were largely swept aside. The infant satire industry became established, launching David Frost and, more importantly, the magazine *Private Eye*—still the most effective chronicle of British misdeeds in high places. Even the government report into the Profumo affair was saucily written, with paragraph headings that read like a novel: " 'He's a liar,' " " 'The swimming pool,' " "The 'darling' letter" and "Paul Mann takes a holiday." Mr. Profumo was unfortunate to make his mistake at a time when Britain was ripe for a scandal. He has now been partly forgiven as a result of charitable work, and recently received a high civil honor.

Cross St. James's Street here, to Brooks's Club opposite. This was built in 1778 for the Whig politicians who, led by Charles James Fox, sympathized with the American Revolution. Outside the club are two lead water butts, now used to grow shrubs. Part the foliage and you'll see molded in the lead a significant date for the Whigs—1776. Also shown is a scene of St. George killing the dragon, symbolizing the defeat of tyranny by the patron saint of England. The American revolutionaries were regarded as fellow Englishmen by radicals in England, who looked forward to the day when they too could throw off the rule of King George III. A group of politicians in England advertised a collection of money on behalf of "the widows, orphans and aged parents of our beloved American fellow-subjects, who, faithful to the character of Englishmen, preferring death to slavery, were for that reason only inhumanly murdered by the king's troops at or near Lexington and Concord."

The first-story windows at Brooks's are low enough for passersby to stare in, and this in the early 1780s caused much scandal. For, just behind the windows, famous members of the club were gambling for enormous stakes at faro. One critic wrote, "The whole town as it passes views the dealer and the punters, by means of the candles, and the windows being levelled with the ground." (The word *punter* is still common British slang, meaning "gambler" or "customer.") In 1781 Fox himself, with a partner, won over £4,000 here at faro in one night. Sadly for him, his numerous creditors took this as a sign that he was now worth

*Lead water tank; eighteenth-century English radicals
celebrate the American Revolution, St. James's Street*

threatening. Bailiffs converged on his nearby house,
carted off his property and held it for ransom.

Go 40 yards farther down St. James's Street (in the
direction of the palace gate house), then turn right and
go through the covered passage into Blue Ball Yard,
one of the most pleasant and unexpected corners of
this district. The yard probably got its name from the
sign of a neighboring pub or house in the eighteenth
century. It is gaslit and paved with flagstones which
slope towards the center, for drainage. The two-story
buildings on the left side were almost certainly built in
1741–42 as wine vaults and stables for an aristocrat

named Francis Godolphin. The first story, where horses and coaches were once kept, is now used as a garage; some of the wooden doors are old and irregular, but they are massively fortified. Above the former stables is a single residential story with a sharply angled roof, more reminiscent of a country cottage than an urban yard. Shrubs, tomatoes and flowers grow in pots along the gallery outside the second story.

Go back into St. James's Street, turn right and after 30 yards you will come to St. James's Place. Go in, and after a few yards turn left into the courtyard by the entrance to Dukes Hotel. The entrance itself is garishly decorated, but the courtyard, largely hidden from the road outside, has a wall delightfully covered by climbing plants. Amid the greenery are two gas lamps.

Return to St. James's Place. This street was laid out in the 1680s and 1690s, and some of its original buildings survive. No. 11, on the far side, was the scene of a violent quarrel in 1698, when the owner was erecting outbuildings in his garden. Neighbors, belonging to the lordly Godolphin family, objected that their privacy was being invaded, and threatened the workmen "with a pistol ready cocked." The present building at no. 11 was put up in the early 1780s, though it has been altered since. In 1820 it became the home of a successful cartoonist, whose influence is still evident. His name was Robert Cruikshank, and he, with his brother George, did the original "Tom and Jerry" cartoons. These cartoons appeared in 1820–21, in a series called "Life in London." The heroes of the drawings were not cat and mouse; they were two wild young men-about-town. "Jerry" was thought at the time to be modeled on Robert Cruikshank himself, and "Tom" on George. Tom and Jerry were shown in fashionable and outrageous scenes—eyeing the stylish courtesans of Covent Garden, meeting "Flashy Nance," the whore who could outdrink a sailor, and cutting a figure in a gin shop, where "blue ruin," a mixture of gin and fruit cordial, was a favorite drink of the day. Especially popular was a cartoon that showed Tom and Jerry, attended by two hopeful and elaborately dressed young prostitutes, playing a practical joke on a "charley." (Charleys were the predecessors of bobbies—watchmen, often elderly, who stood in sentry boxes at night and tried to keep order in the streets.) Jerry and the two women look on while a grinning Tom pushes over a watchman's box from behind. The charley falls forward, followed by the sentry box, which pins him helplessly to the ground.

The cartoons were a huge success. "Tom and Jerry" hats appeared in London. Pirate editions of the drawings were sold across the Atlantic, making the phrase "Tom and Jerry" widely known in America. Tom and Jerry behavior was also copied, with serious results for charleys. There was an outbreak of charley-baiting throughout London; one observer noted that even in a quiet suburb "the watchman's box was on several occasions toppled over on its slumbering inmate, by parties of young bloods fresh from flowing bowls of punch. . . ." Another critic claimed that Tom and Jerry "had a great deal to answer for in the way of leading soft-headed young men astray."

George Cruikshank had already become famous as a political cartoonist; he was especially fond of showing the Prince Regent (later George IV) with careful attention to the Prince's vast waist and rear. The more scandalous of these cartoons were so wounding that a secret royal payment of £100 was made to the artist in 1820, in return for a promise "not to caricature His Majesty in any immoral situation." George Cruikshank was probably more radical than his brother Robert, but he enjoyed the expensive and dissipated way of life shown in the "Tom and Jerry" cartoons. According to his publisher, he was addicted to "late hours, blue ruin and dollies." Later in the nineteenth century, when the shocking Georgian court had been replaced with Queen Victoria's propriety, George Cruikshank publicly renounced drink and became a temperance campaigner. Many other Victorians were ashamed to look back on their own pre-Victorian pasts, and the novelist Thackeray had fun imagining an innocent Victorian child questioning its now-respectable grandparents about their doings in the heyday of Tom and Jerry:

> Grandmamma, did you wear such a dress as that when you danced? . . . There was very little of it, grandmamma! Did grandpapa kill many watchmen when he was a young man, and frequent thieves, gin-shops, cock-fights and the ring before you married him? He is very much changed. He seems a gentlemanly old boy now.

Nos. 13 and 14, a little farther along St. James's Place, are the best preserved of the small buildings in the street. No. 14 is a late-seventeenth-century structure, though its front has been given a later coat of stucco (a plaster made of lime, portland cement and sand). In front of the flat first story, two thin iron pillars support the bay front of the second and third, producing a ramshackle elegance.

Opposite these houses the street opens into a wide space where horses and carriages could comfortably turn. On the far side is no. 28, a magnificent flat-fronted town house, dating mainly from the late eighteenth century. There is an intricately patterned fanlight above the door, and outside is a superb array of antique lighting equipment. On each side of the entrance is a conical torch extinguisher in iron. Above are two metal loops which once held the glass globes of oil lamps. And, standing out from the wall, is a functioning light of the sort which, in the early nineteenth century, made both torches and oil lamps obsolete—gas.

The blue plaque at no. 28 mentions that this was once the home of a politician named William Huskisson. In an age when several of his eminent colleagues were notorious for drinking and dueling, Huskisson was a more sober character. The best-remembered episode of his life is his departure from it. In 1830, he attended a ceremony to open the Liverpool-to-Manchester railway. But, while anxiously scrambling out of the way of an approaching locomotive called "The Rocket," he fell out of a carriage and his leg was run over. He died in great pain a few hours later.

Next door to Huskisson's narrow and elegant brick house is a building in a very different style, no. 27, Spencer House. Far wider, it is built of yellowish stone with flat pilasters and classical columns. The architect, John Vardy, was originally hired to build a great house here by one Henry Bromley, the first Baron Montfort. But the plan fell through: Bromley got into financial trouble, called his lawyer, carefully read over his will and then shot himself before the lawyer had time to leave. Later, in the 1760s, Vardy found another client, John Spencer (later Earl Spencer). This young man had fallen in love before being of an age to marry; his wedding took place on the day after he came of age and yet in one of the rooms of this house he commissioned a painting showing a secret marriage. Look through the window just beyond the door at the glitteringly gilded ceiling.

Behind (to the south of) Spencer House was once Cleveland House, a mansion owned by Barbara Villiers, Duchess of Cleveland. She was one of the greediest and most notorious of Charles II's mistresses, and was also extremely beautiful. During the great plague of 1665, Samuel Pepys, while terrified of dying, had a dream about holding Barbara in his arms. He concluded that if dying meant entering a dreamlike existence of that kind, death wouldn't be such a bad thing after all.

Go across the road to where St. James's Place bends to the right and runs uphill for about 100 yards. At the top of the little hill, on the left, is a modern building, no. 21. This site was once the northwest corner of Barbara Villiers's garden, and in 1956, when the present building was being erected, interesting traces of her luxurious life-style were found here. A pit—nearly thirteen feet deep and more than thirteen feet in diameter at the top—was discovered; its sides sloped inwards as they descended, and were lined with bricks. This was an icehouse, built in 1668 or soon afterwards, and at the time known more prettily as a "snow well." In winter, ice and snow were packed into it; deep below ground, they remained frozen for much of the summer, enabling wine and food to be lowered in and chilled. This idea was brought from Italy and France, and probably was first used in England in the early 1660s, soon after the restoration of Charles II. The first royal snow well, built not far from here, was eagerly saluted by a court poet, Edmund Waller:

Yonder the harvest of cold months laid up,
Gives a fresh coolness to the royal cup;
There ice like crystal, firm and never lost,
Tempers hot July with December's frost.
Winter's dark prison; whence he cannot fly,
Though the warm Spring, his enemy, grows nigh.
Strange! that extremes should thus preserve the snow,
High on the Alps, and in deep caves below.

Four kinds of old lighting equipment—gaslight, oil light,
fanlight and torch extinguisher, St. James's Place

Five snow wells were built for the King on the sites of nos. 22–25 St. James's Place, but they seem not to have worked satisfactorily; before 1700 they were allowed to fall into disrepair.

Next door, at the end of St. James's Place and looking down the hill, is no. 20—still gaslit at the front. Go past it to the small blind alley that runs from the right of the street. Here, 3 yards past the door of no. 19, look at the tiny window about 6 feet from the ground. It measures approximately 11 × 10 inches but across it is set a stout iron bar—to keep out any little Artful Dodgers. No. 19 also has some fragile-looking but attractive bow windows.

Come back down St. James's Place, passing (on the right) the small alley which dives under no. 21 and comes up again at the edge of Green Park. Follow the road around to the left, until you emerge again into St. James's Street. Cross the street and go right; the block just beyond King Street contains three of London's best-known and oldest specialty shops: Lobb's the shoemakers, Lock's the men's hatters and the wine merchants Berry Bros. and Rudd. All three serve the royal court, and I confess that I expected their staff to be fearfully grand—many posh English shops depend on intimidation to impress customers. Instead I found quiet manners and an interest in getting the product right according to the producer's own high standards as well as those of the customer.

On the door of Lobb's, at no. 9 St. James's Street, are wooden plaques painted with the insignia of two past customers, "His Imperial Majesty the Emperor of Ethiopia" and "His Majesty the King of Thailand." In a little window to the right of the entrance is an excerpt from a Victorian publication, recording that Lobb's won the only gold medal for boot making at the Paris Exhibition of 1867: "The jurors declared they never saw such beautiful workmanship and style." The business has existed since 1850. The founder, John Lobb, was a Cornishman who brought back the capital to open his London store after a successful stay in Australia, where he had designed a "prospector's boot" for the gold diggers—of ordinary appearance but with a hollow heel for nuggets and gold dust. Lobb's descendants still run the firm.

A few yards farther, at no. 6, is Lock's, which claims

to be the oldest surviving hatter's business in the world. It has been in St. James's Street since the late seventeenth century, and in its present building since 1765. The plain and dignified shop front has delicate and slightly irregular bars dividing the windows; below these a grille of hefty iron reaches down to the sidewalk, allowing light to the basement while keeping out thieves. Notice, too, the ancient (and valued) dents in the door. Always on show in the left-hand window are some of Lock's tall hats from the early nineteenth century—similar, by the way, to those shown in the "Tom and Jerry" cartoons. The two light-colored hats are called "beavers," the dark ones "silk." In the right-hand window is a three-cornered ("tricorn") hat, of a type well known in Britain and America from eighteenth-century paintings. These antiques aren't for sale. Lock's still makes some military caps (you will see specimens from bygone ages in the window); famous British warriors who have been customers here include the commanders in the Napoleonic wars, Admiral Lord Nelson and the Duke of Wellington.

In recent years the hatting industry has been trying to recover from the lean years of the late 1960s and early 1970s, when elaborate male hairstyles often replaced the hat. When I was speaking to him, Mr. Stephenson, the manager here, glanced out of his second-story window and estimated that only about one in twenty of the men in sight was wearing a hat—and this is conservative St. James's. But casual male headwear seems to be making a comeback.

Like its two eminent neighbors, Lock's values its American connections. Customers from the United States in recent years have included Elliott Gould, Gregory Peck, Senator Daniel P. Moynihan and the late Vice President Nelson Rockefeller.

Ten yards farther, at no. 3 St. James's Street, is the wine shop of Berry Bros. and Rudd. The alleyway beside it leads to a charming eighteenth-century courtyard, as we shall see in a moment. First, though, look at the front of the shop. On weekends and in the evenings only the arched tops of the first-story windows are visible, the rest being hidden by thick wooden shutters which date, like the building itself, from the eighteenth century. Underneath their glossy black paint the shutters have numerous scars, some of them dating from 1940 when a stick of bombs hit the area. Among those killed was a sentry outside St. James's Palace, 100 yards away.

On a weekday, look through the windows at the austerely elegant interior. The ceiling is low, the floor is of bare boards and there are no modern wine bottles on display. But to the right are black, antique bottles, and also a display of miniature bottles which are scarcely an inch high. These miniatures were made in the 1920s when Queen Mary, wife of King George V and a compulsive collector, employed one of the firm's directors to equip a dollhouse with its own cellar of wine. Great ingenuity was used in producing the tiny bottles and their labels, and in filling them with the corresponding wines by pipette—the necks of the bottles being too narrow otherwise to allow in even small drops of wine.

Also on the right side of the shop is a table where customers browse undisturbed through the firm's list. Prices, I found, were not exorbitant, though the firm is known around the world. (For one thing, its name is on the label of every bottle of Cutty Sark whiskey.) But notice, as the firm's list points out, that the prices quoted do not include V.A.T. (Value Added Tax). By a useful arrangement, wine—whether a few bottles or a number of cases—can be bought from afar; the firm will then store it on the customer's behalf, in the correct conditions and for a minimal charge. Visitors planning to visit London months, or even years ahead can thus have their wine waiting—and improving—for them in Berry's store.

From the ceiling of the shop hang two weighing beams, both from the eighteenth century. The smaller one is still in use for a custom which has existed here since the 1760s: weighing clients. Until the late nineteenth century few scales were available elsewhere for personal measurement, and many grand people came here for the purpose. Some insisted on being weighed naked, for greater accuracy. The records, handwritten and carefully preserved in the shop in large ledgers, note very properly that in such cases the shop was closed at the time. Clothing and diet were also noted, sometimes in obsessive detail. (Weight watching was thought an important guide to health; also, in an age of aristocratic indulgence, there was a widespread and often reasonable dread of getting fat.) One nineteenth-century grandee, the 4th Baron Rivers, had his weight recorded here nearly five hundred times. For example: "1864, July 27th, 12 stone 4 lbs. at 1:30; 12 stone 5 lbs. at 2 p.m. after two chops and a pint of sherry."

Among the most interesting records in the ledgers are those recalling the weight of George III's sons, the gigantic Hanoverian princes sometimes called "Queen Victoria's wicked uncles." The Duke of Wellington once referred to these men as "the damnedest mill-stones that were ever hanged round the neck of any government." Their measurements help to explain his remark. The second eldest of the royal brothers, the Duke of York, weighed 204 1/2 pounds (in shoes) in 1800. He distinguished himself as a reformer at the head of the British army until 1809, when it was discovered that his mistress, Mary Anne Clarke, had appointed officers in return for bribes. The Duke had to resign his military post in a cloud of scandal. His brother William (later King William IV) weighed 189 pounds (in boots) in 1800. He was a man of lively appetites, fathering at least ten children, none of them legitimate. Look at the top of the gate house of the palace, and you'll see a large clock restored during his reign, bearing the letters WR—William Rex (King)—and the date, 1832. Another brother, the imposing and tyrannical Duke of Cumberland, weighed 189 pounds (in boots) in 1799. More about him later; two of his personal enemies were to die in appalling circumstances, and many in England were relieved when he was sent away to become King of Hanover. A more popular brother, the Duke of Cambridge, weighed 226 1/2 pounds in 1822. Queen Victoria's father, the Duke of Kent, weighed 232 1/2 pounds.

The oldest and most important of the brothers is the only one not to have his weight recorded here: George, Prince of Wales, Prince Regent and later King George IV. His vast proportions and prospective health were a matter of national importance (and of international satire), and were perhaps too sensitive to be entrusted even to the discreetly guarded registers of no. 3. But the Prince was a customer. So too was his satirical opponent, George Cruikshank, and one of Cruikshank's most famous cartoons shows a massive, blubbery sea creature with the unmistakable royal face—the Prince of Whales, of course.

Go down the alleyway to the left of Berry's. Its walls are paneled for the first 6 feet from the ground; above that, on the right, you can see how the wall is built with timber filled in with brick. (A friend of mine who sings discovered that the acoustics are excellent here.) About halfway along the alley on the right is a modern plaque that was made in San Antonio. It records that the building contained the Texan legation between 1842 and 1845, at the time when Texas was an independent republic. Mr. Anthony Berry, the chairman of Berry Bros., who takes an enlightened interest in the history of the building, believes that the legation was on the second story on the side next to the alley. The wine business was suffering in the general depression of the 1840s ("the hungry '40s"), and the American tenants were welcome.

At the end of the alley is Pickering Place, a tiny courtyard named after William Pickering who, in the 1730s, constructed most of the buildings that survive, including the one occupied by Berry's. Look at the intricate eighteenth-century doorcases, in wood, at nos. 3 and 4. There is no rear entry to these buildings, and if you look through the windows you will see that their rooms are very small. Pickering was squeezing the maximum number of buildings into his little plot. High above the entries to nos. 3 and 4 is a superbly tangled mass of iron drainpipes.

On a weekday, look in briefly at the fourth window on the right, counting from the entrance to the courtyard (bearing in mind that this belongs to a private office of Berry Bros.). Still on the walls of the little room is the original paneling, and above the fireplace are antique port bottles, arranged to show the development of their shapes. The earlier bottles are bulbous with long necks; the modern cylindrical shape emerged around 1760. (It was discovered that port improved with long keeping in the bottle; cylindrical bottles could easily be kept stacked on their sides while the bulbous type could not.)

For the weekend, folding wooden shutters (instead of curtains or blinds) are drawn across the windows inside. Shutters like this were made well into the nineteenth century and are now a valued feature of an old building. They gave security in a way that curtains obviously didn't. They also provided better insulation and lasted far longer. Underneath Pickering Place is part of the cellars of Berry Bros. (Other cellars of the firm stretch below St. James's Street.) In this section of the cellars, Napoleon III is believed to have plotted his return to France during his exile in the 1840s.

Before going to St. James's Palace, the last area of the walk, have a look at the only surviving low alley in the neighborhood. To reach it, go back down the passage into St. James's Street, turn right, and right again at the first corner, into King Street. Thirty yards along King Street on the right is an entry under an archway with its own gaslight. This is Crown Passage, an island of working-class life and unpretentious businesses. Along it you will find several sandwich bars, the kind of place that visitors seldom use, but known by local office workers for some of the best values in town. There is also a hardware store and a dealer in coins. Nearby, in King Street, are far grander antique and coin businesses: Christie's and Spink's. No doubt some of the traders who set up in Crown Passage hope that one day it will take on the tone of King Street and become a genteel shopping precinct. At the far end is a pub, The Red Lion, with pleasant models of lions' heads above the first story. (There are many pubs with the same names in London and elsewhere.) The flat front of the upper stories suggests that the building has been here since the early nineteenth century or before.

Crown Passage has existed in something like its present form since at least the 1790s, when at the end adjoining King Street there was a "rookery" (a stronghold of slum-dwellers and criminals who "rooked"—cheated—people). There were similar slums and alleys to the east, the direction away from St. James's Street. Part of this area was described in the mid-nineteenth century as a "low den of infamy." Haymarket, the teeming headquarters of Victorian prostitution, was less than half a mile away to the northeast.

Leaving Crown Passage by the far end, you'll come out into Pall Mall. This street is dominated now by ponderous Victorian buildings containing gentlemen's clubs. In the seventeenth century it was a far quieter place, and got its name from a game played here by

royalty with a wooden ball ("pell" or "pall") and mallet ("mell" or "mall"). King James I may have introduced the game to England in 1603 or soon afterwards; he advised his short-lived son Henry to become fairly good at it: "The exercises that I would have you to use (although but moderately, not making a craft of them) are running, leaping, wrestling, fencing, archery, pall mall...." Expertise was to be avoided, because it was thought by aristocrats to be vulgar—the mark of one who had to earn a living.

The poet and flatterer, Edmund Waller, who wrote the lines about Charles II's snow well, also produced some excited verse about Charles's skill at pall mall. According to Waller, a ball struck by the King went like a shot from a culverin (a long cannon):

> Here a well-polished mall gives us the joy
> To see our prince his matchless force employ . . .
> No sooner has he touched the flying ball,
> But 'tis already more than half the mall,
> And such a fury from his arm has got
> As from a smoking culverin 'twere shot.

Cross Pall Mall and go to the right (into Cleveland Row), to the great gate-house tower of St. James's Palace. The tower is of faded red brick, has four stories and stands astride a pair of massive and battered wooden gates. At each corner are octagonal turrets, crowned with battlements. This is the grandest part of the palace to have survived from the time of Henry VIII. On each side of the wooden gates is a small doorway; look closely at the one on the left, and in its top right corner you can just make out worn figures cut in the stone. There is a crown and below it a Tudor rose. This badge was formed by combining the rival red and white roses, emblems of the great warring families of fifteenth-century England—the houses of Lancaster and York. Henry VIII was the son of a victorious Lancastrian father, Henry Tudor (Henry VII), but his mother was from the other side—Elizabeth of York. The Tudor rose, when painted, shows a red rose embracing a white.

Close to you is a sentry box, normally manned by a soldier from one of the elite Guards regiments. The

Crown Passage

guardsmen are often recruited for their powerful physiques. Their officers, however, are chosen partly for their social background; it's understood that an officer without a private income would be unlikely to afford the large informal expenses of life in the Guards. The sentries here are guardsmen, not officers; their job, as well as being decorative, is to protect the members of the Royal Family who live in, or close to, St. James's Palace.

As you pass the wooden gates, look at the window directly above. This was once a crucial vantage point of Henry VIII's domestic fortress. Now it has lace curtains; behind them, in the summer, I have seen something which looks remarkably like a tomato plant. At night in the eighteenth century, this spot blazed with oil lights; you can see the four horizontal brackets which stand out beside the gate. Now there are electric lights in the metal loops that once held the globes of the oil lamps. More oil-lamp standards rise from the railings a few yards farther along. Before you pass them, look closely at the height of the small door just to the right of the gates. It rises to a shallow pointed arch, but even here it is only 6 feet high. Guards, like the population in general, have grown taller since the days of Henry VIII.

A few yards past the gate house is a huge window: this belongs to the Chapel Royal, the setting for some passionate and some comical events, as we shall see shortly. On the sidewalk are the standards of gas lamps put up in the 1820s. Near their base they have the insignia of King George IV, who reigned from 1820 to 1830. The first public gaslights in London were set up in 1807, near here in Pall Mall. George Cruikshank greeted them with a cartoon showing passersby retching from the gas, a bird dropping dead from the sky and a gassed cat slithering helplessly down a roof. Fifty yards past the window of the chapel, just beyond the third gas lamp and half-hidden around a corner of the wall, are two metal fire marks from the period around 1800, making clear that even royalty needed to be insured with private fire brigades. One of the plaques was put up by St. Martin's insurance company; it shows the saint on horseback.

This wing of St. James's Palace was fitted out in 1795 to receive an unfortunate royal bride, Caroline of

Brunswick. Her fiancé was the prince who later became George IV. Sadly for her, George was already married, secretly, to a woman named Maria Fitzherbert. Maria was a Catholic, and if George had married her publicly he would have lost his claim to the throne; even today the heir to the throne is not allowed to marry a Catholic. George was intermittently attached to Maria for many years, but ran very heavily into debt; by 1794 he owed over £600,000. An open, official marriage with someone else would help to overcome this, because Parliament would then vote George an increased allowance to meet his new marital responsibilities. So Caroline, George's cousin, was summoned from Germany.

When she arrived in London, George was taken aback by the appearance of the ample, cheerful and dark young woman. When they met, his first words were not to her but to an attendant: "I am not well. Pray get me a glass of brandy." Caroline was given as her close companion Lady Jersey, George's current mistress and a willing spy, who relayed parts of Caroline's letters to George's mother. At the wedding in the Chapel Royal, the Archbishop of Canterbury paused deliberately when asking whether anyone knew of an impediment to the marriage. But no one spoke, and George acquired a second wife.

The intimacy of the royal couple did not last long, though a daughter resulted—Charlotte, whose sad death we noted earlier in the walk. In January 1796, just three days after Charlotte was born, her father decided on suicide and drew up a romantic, self-dramatizing will leaving an insulting sum—one shilling—to Charlotte's mother. The rest of the estate, George wrote, was to go to "Maria Fitzherbert, my wife, the wife of my heart and soul . . . my true and real wife, and who is dearer to me, even millions of times dearer to me, than that life I am now going to resign." George directed that after his death a miniature portrait of Maria was to be "placed right upon my heart." When Maria herself came to die, her coffin was to be placed next to his, the adjoining sides removed and the coffins then soldered together.

After the excitement of writing this, George decided instead to live. He and Caroline drifted further apart, and both found comfort elsewhere. Many years later, in 1820, George formally became King, and Caroline returned from abroad to claim her position as Queen of England. George tried to disown her, and had her physically shut out of his Coronation in Westminster Abbey. He also tried to obtain a divorce, and thus created one of the ripest scandals in English history. We shall come to it on the last walk.

Continue along the wall of the palace until you reach the first entrance on the left. Just before turning in, notice the intricate spray of ironwork on the second-story balcony of the house opposite. Inside the palace, in a yard on the right, is a covered walkway, built as part of the royal stables in the 1660s. An important character in this Stable Yard was the royal rat-killer; in 1741 his name was John Gower. His job was highly respected ("an honourable office")—worth £100 a year, a considerable sum. A royal document describes Mr. Gower's handsome coat, which had rats embroidered on the sleeves:

> Received from His Majesty's Great Wardrobe Office a crimson cloth coat lined with blue serge, guarded [edged] with blue velvet and embroidery, richly on back and breast, with His Majesty's letters and crowns, and on the arms with rats and wheatsheaf, being a livery for Mr. John Gower, Rat-Killer in Ordinary to His Majesty.

Another smartly dressed official in the eighteenth century was the herb-strewer, whose job was to perfume the palace: "To Alice Bell, Herb-Strewer to his Majesty, two yards of scarlet cloth for a livery for the year 1716." On the far side of Stable Yard is a tall, imposing stone building, Lancaster House. This was begun in 1825 on the orders of George IV's brother, the Duke of York. The Duke expected to become King on his brother's death, and, in spite of massive debts, was eager to have a grand residence befitting his status. But he died in 1827, three years before his brother, and the unfinished building passed into the hands of his creditors. In this century Lancaster House was given to the nation. Visits are therefore permitted, except during government functions, when the house is sealed off by security men.

The large white building a few yards away across the road from Lancaster House is Clarence House, for

many years the residence of Queen Elizabeth, the
Queen Mother—the widow of the wartime king,
George VI, and perhaps the most popular member of
the Royal Family in recent times. This house, too, was
built to the order of one of George III's sons, William,
Duke of Clarence, later William IV. The architect was
John Nash, designer of slightly shoddy masterpieces.
(More distinguished work of his can be seen a few
hundred yards from here, at the far end of The Mall,
in Carlton House Terrace, a great white cliff of slender
aristocratic houses.)

Unfortunately, regular public access to Ambassa-
dor's Court was ended in 1980, for undisclosed reasons of "security." Standing at the entrance, though,
you can still see on the far side of the court the wall
of the Chapel Royal. Inside the chapel, in January
1649, King Charles I attended service on the morning
of his execution. Defeated in the Civil War by the
forces of Parliament, he had at first been spared. But
when he raised more forces to reopen the war, the parliamentary chief, Oliver Cromwell, lost patience and
said that to have any further dealings with him was "to
meddle with an accursed thing." Charles was put on
trial; he refused to recognize the court and was sentenced to death. His dignity on the scaffold is a favorite theme of sentimental writers in England, being
easier to dramatize than the deaths of countless ordinary soldiers in the Civil Wars. According to one of his
attendants, Charles asked for an extra shirt on the January morning, not wishing to shiver and seem afraid.
After reaching the scaffold in Whitehall, he made some
grave utterances, as the ax lay ready in his view. Twice
he broke off in alarm when spectators got close to the
ax, calling out in fear that they would blunt it and
make his death more painful: "Hurt not the ax that may
hurt me"; "Take heed of the ax, pray take heed of the
ax!" In the event, only one stroke of it was needed.

Eleven years later the dead King's son, Charles II, re-
gained the throne and began to spend more relaxed
hours in the Chapel Royal. The Republicans had been
religious enthusiasts; Charles II and his court were the
opposite. One preacher here, Dr. South, noticed that
during a sermon all the congregation, including King
Charles, was asleep. South stopped, changed his tone

and called out to one of the sleepers, the powerful Lord Lauderdale: "My Lord, I am sorry to interrupt your repose, but I must beg you will not snore so loud, lest you awaken His Majesty."

At the end of Charles II's life, a courtier with puritanical leanings, John Evelyn, was shocked by the way Sunday was spent at St. James's Palace:

> I am never to forget the inexpressible luxury, and profaneness, gaming and all dissolution, and as it were total forgetfulness of God (it being Sunday evening) which this day sennight [a week ago] I was witness of; the King, sitting and toying with his concubines Portsmouth, Cleveland and Mazarine etc., a French boy singing love songs in that glorious gallery, whilst about twenty of the great courtiers and other dissolute persons were [playing] at basset round a large table, a bank of at least 2,000 in gold before them.

"Six days after," Evelyn noted with satisfaction, "all was in the dust." King Charles II was dead.

Fifteen years later, in 1700, the Chapel Royal had become a place for fashionable people to show off and flirt—much like St. James's Church in Piccadilly. A certain Bishop Burnet disapproved, and complained to Princess Anne (niece of the late Charles II) about the amorous "ogling and sighing" that went on in the chapel. He wanted the wooden pews to be built up, so that the worshippers would no longer be able to look at each other. He got his way, and a satirical poem appeared, hinting that the Bishop had simply been anxious to get the pretty women to gaze at him instead. In the poem the Bishop is "quoted" as complaining to the Princess about the flirtation in chapel, and then as saying:

> These practices, Madam, my preaching disgrace;
> Shall Laymen enjoy the just rights of my place?
> Then all may lament my condition so hard,
> Who thrash in the pulpit without a reward.
>   Therefore, pray condescend
>   Such disorders to end,
> And to the ripe vineyards the labourers send,
> To build up the seats that the beauties may see
> The face of no brawling pretender but me.

The Princess, by the man's importunity pressed,
Though she laughed at his reasons, allowed his
    request:
And now Britain's nymphs, in a Protestant reign,
Are locked up at prayers like the virgins in Spain.

Keeping Clarence House on your left, go through
the great iron gates into The Mall. When you reach it,
look back over the wall to the left, to the late seventeenth-century section of St. James's Palace which joins
Clarence House and runs parallel to The Mall. Near the
east (right) end of this wing is the room where a son
was born in 1688 to King James II, the Catholic brother of Charles II. Many Protestants were eager for James
to be succeeded by one of his grown-up daughters,
Mary or Anne, who were Protestants. But when James
had a son by Mary of Modena, his second wife, an Italian Catholic, it seemed that Catholic rule might become permanent. So, as a result of wishful thinking or
pure lying, many people were persuaded that the baby
was not the child of James and Mary but had been
smuggled into Mary's chamber in a warming pan. According to different versions, Mary had either miscar-
ried or not been pregnant at all. Smuggling in the child
at the right time would certainly have been difficult.
There were sixty-seven people present in Mary's bed-
chamber, many of them high officials of state checking
that the birth was indeed genuine. One critic of the
story wrote that:

> the warming pan is no feasible project, unless you break
> the back of the child to put it in; moreover, as this is sup-
> posed to be a tender infant, just reeking and wet from its
> mother's womb, in that tender state it would either have
> cried out in the passage, or have been still and dead, and
> in the variety of motions of tossing it up and down, it
> would have been a perfect jelly.

But the rumor remained lively and encouraged the
Protestant forces which ejected King James from England a few months later. The baby grew up to be
known as "The Pretender." Based in France, he inspired the Scottish Rebellion of 1715. His son, "Bonnie
Prince Charlie" (also called "The Young Pretender"),
led the Scottish uprising of 1745.
    Turn left into The Mall, and turn left again at the

next corner into Marlborough Road. About 100 yards along is an opening into another section of St. James's Palace, Friary Court. A brick balcony with ornamental battlements runs the length of the far side. Here, on the morning after the death of a monarch, the successor is proclaimed to the crowds below. One of the most anxiously awaited of all royal proclamations occurred on the balcony in 1837. That story will end the walk.

In the 1830s royalty had reached a crisis. There had not been a profoundly impressive monarch for centuries, since the death of Queen Elizabeth in 1603. Of the most recent kings George III had been mad (in his last years he thought he was an animal in Noah's Ark), George IV had been wildly scandalous, and William IV ("Silly Billy") was little better. Next in line was the promising schoolgirl Princess Victoria—unless she were to die. But many were afraid that she would die, because the person who stood to benefit, the second in line of succession, was the reckless and vicious Duke of Cumberland.

Cumberland's record was dreadful, and when he appeared in the streets he was usually hissed. As a politician he once bribed men to produce an anti-Catholic demonstration and had been caught using bribery at a parliamentary election. In private life he had scandalized a French nunnery by making eyes at the nuns and trying to kiss the abbess. On another occasion his valet, a Corsican named Sellis, had attacked him and inflicted serious wounds; it was said that Sellis had found Cumberland in bed with his wife. Sellis was found shortly afterwards with his throat cut, probably a suicide. Cumberland's name was later linked with that of a Lady Graves; her husband too was found with his throat cut. Cumberland, in middle age, also tried to rape the wife of the Lord Chancellor in her own home. This was the man who stood to become King of England if Victoria were to die, and whose unpopularity could perhaps have brought monarchy to an end. Rumors that he wished to kill Victoria were so powerful that Cumberland had to issue a discreet denial; he stated in the House of Lords that he was willing to shed his last drop of blood for "that innocent person" Victoria. But in 1837 he inherited the throne of the little German kingdom of Hanover and was obliged to go.

He tried to delay his departure from England, only to be told by the Duke of Wellington, "Go—before you are pelted out!" Reluctantly, Cumberland went.

So it was that on June 21, 1837, Victoria, freed from the shadow of her sinister uncle, stood at the balcony here to be proclaimed Queen at the age of eighteen. She looked pale and anxious and, out of respect for the dead William IV, was dressed "in deep mourning, with a white tippet [cape], white cuffs and a border of white lace under a small black bonnet, which was placed far back upon her head, exhibiting her light hair in front simply parted over the forehead." After blasts from trumpets and cannons and intense cheering from the crowd below the balcony, Victoria was overcome. She turned to her mother and wept.

In her reign Victoria was often generous and enlightened, especially behind the scenes. She collaborated with Florence Nightingale to stop the custom of reducing soldiers' pay when they fell sick. She insisted that her Indian subjects not be treated arrogantly by British administrators. In private life, she intervened to help rehabilitate Mary Ann Evans (the brilliant novelist George Eliot) after she had been partly ostracized for living with a (technically) married man. Victoria made mistakes but her general decency was obvious. She succeeded in largely abolishing the memory of her wicked Hanoverian predecessors. The present Royal Family still profits from the respect which she earned.

London's Latin Quarter: Chelsea

○

For Londoners, "Chelsea" means above all the King's Road, a long, fashionable, crowded street just to the west of central London and a few hundred yards north of the Thames. Here the fashion designer Mary Quant opened her first shop in 1955. Imitators soon appeared, and the King's Road became a main artery of Swinging London in the 1960s. Quant's shop is now gone, but the road has held its magnetism for young people. They come to display their new clothes and poses—so don't be afraid to stare!

Only a few of the younger people on the sidewalk actually live in Chelsea. Housing in the area is wildly expensive. A spacious house in the most favored part of Chelsea is likely to cost over half a million pounds. In the 1970s Mick Jagger and Keith Richards lived here; their neighbors included Paul Getty, a duchess and Mrs. Margaret Thatcher. Most of our walk will be in this residential section, away from the King's Road and close to the river. Here you will find quiet eighteenth-century terraces, some built in a grand sweep to overlook the Thames, others clustered around a little street wide enough only for a single horse-drawn carriage.

Chelsea has been a chic address since the early sixteenth century, when Thomas More built himself a large house near the river. As Henry VIII's Lord Chancellor, More had a set of uniformed boatmen to take him downstream to court. Henry visited More at Chelsea, liked the area and in 1536, shortly after arranging More's execution, unsentimentally began to build himself a home here. King Henry's manor house became the residence of two of his six queens. Many years later, its last occupant was Sir Hans Sloane, an eighteenth-century society physician. Sloane demolished More's nearby house, but to his credit arranged for the building of an elegant riverside terrace, Cheyne (pronounced "chainy") Walk. Sloane also saved the Physic Garden, a walled sanctuary for rare and medicinal plants—which, like Cheyne Walk, still survives. On Sloane's death in 1753, much of his Chelsea estate

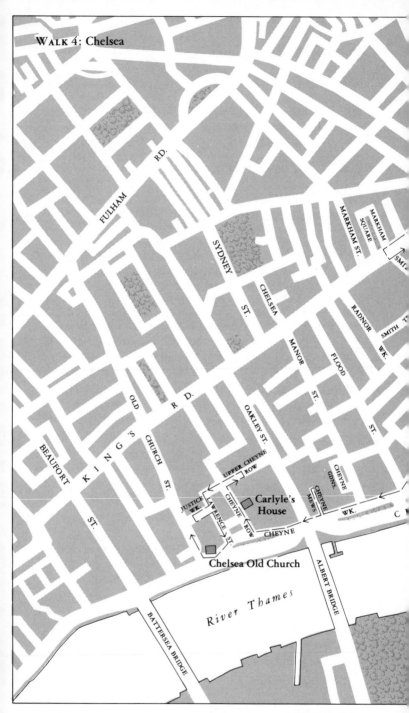

passed to his daughter, Elizabeth. She married an aristocrat named Cadogan, and the Cadogan family have remained landlords here to the present day.

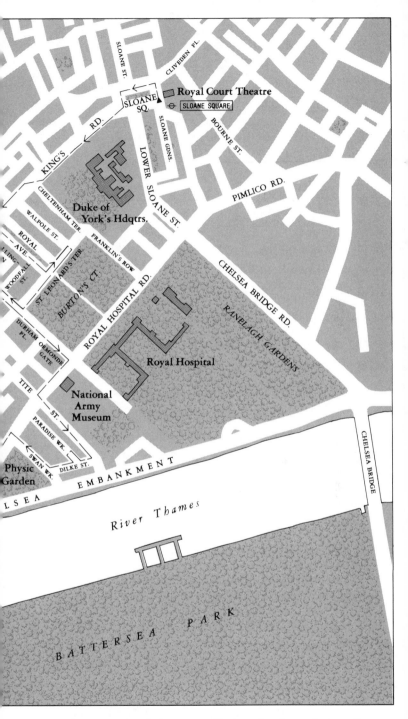

In the nineteenth century Chelsea had a colony of famous writers and artists, British, Irish and American. George Eliot, the novelist, lived on Cheyne Walk. Oscar Wilde, the exotic bisexual playwright, spent his greatest years nearby in Tite Street. In the same street the artist James McNeill Whistler built his ideal house, only to lose it within months because of a disastrous lawsuit. John Singer Sargent painted his lavish portraits of society ladies in a neighboring studio. Oscar Wilde teased one of them from his doorstep as she passed on her way to a sitting with Sargent—dressed as Lady Macbeth.

One house especially symbolizes Chelsea's bohemian past: the riverside home of Dante Gabriel Rossetti, the mid-Victorian painter and poet. Here numerous models and mistresses drifted in and out, helping themselves to large supplies of money stuffed handily into a drawer. The place was a ménage inside and a menagerie outside with Rossetti's expensive and impractical zoo. Especially lovable, as we shall see, were the pet armadillos—skillful little miners with no sense of property boundaries. Rossetti's peacocks, which flew screeching up into the neighbors' trees, caused serious complaints; so the Cadogan estate wrote, and still writes, a special clause into its leases that strictly forbids the keeping of peacocks.

Leave Sloane Square tube station and go a few steps to the right, to the entrance of the Royal Court Theatre. The sidewalk here is a favorite spot for social display, especially on summer evenings when theatergoers are arriving. In the 1950s the Royal Court added to Chelsea's bohemian reputation by launching the play *Look Back in Anger*, one of the first signs of the revolt against English postwar dullness and conservatism. The playwright, John Osborne, published a famous letter explaining why he hated England, and completed the act by emigrating. He returned not long afterwards, having secured his reputation as an Angry Young Man, and wrote the excellent screenplay for the film *Tom Jones*.

In a moment you'll be leaving Sloane Square by an exit on its farthest side, almost directly opposite the tube station. But look first at Sloane Street, which leaves the square to the right, just twenty yards beyond the theater. This spot is now entirely urban, and it is hard to imagine that the road here was once desolate at night and dreaded by travelers from London.

A few yards down that road to the right was Bloody Bridge, over a stream called the Westbourne, and people who had to cross it made an attractive target for highwaymen. Robbery was so common in the eighteenth century that some travelers used to carry two purses—one, well hidden, containing most of their money and another one to be surrendered to highwaymen. The Westbourne, like other London streams, now runs underground to the Thames; at Sloane Square tube station it crosses the railway tracks in a great iron case.

Walk around Sloane Square to the far side. Of the two exits there, take the one on the left, King's Road. You will then have on your right the large and respected general store, Peter Jones. This business was founded in Chelsea in 1871 by Mr. Jones, a Welshman; in 1906 it was bought by another Welsh emigré, John Lewis, whose company still owns it. To complete the purchase, Lewis walked here from central London with twenty £1000 bank-notes in his pockets—a colossal sum that, luckily for him, wasn't detected by any twentieth-century highwaymen.

Now walk up King's Road for a few minutes before turning away into the quieter and more obviously historic parts of Chelsea. The name of the road comes from King Charles II, who in the late seventeenth century used it as a private track between his courts at London and Hampton.

Fifty yards beyond Peter Jones, on the left, are hefty iron railings; go almost to the end of them, then look through at the stylish classical building, with columns and portico, that overlooks a large lawn. The building, called the Duke of York's Headquarters, was begun in 1801 as a school for the children of soldiers. Children still play on the lawn, but the buildings nearby are now barracks. The school was founded by the Duke of York—George III's second son—who was in some ways an effective military reformer. During the Napoleonic Wars he tried to abolish the old practice of buying military commissions for prestige or to gain access to valuable military stores. Utterly unsuitable people had become officers in this way, and the Duke called for the resignations of all colonels under the age of twenty and captains under the age of twelve. His reforming, however, was interrupted in 1809 when it emerged that his own mistress had been selling commissions. The Duke was forced to resign in disgrace.

Pass Cheltenham Terrace, the next turn on the left; a few steps farther, on the right-hand side of King's Road, the row of Chelsea boutiques begins. Look above the modernized and rather brash shop fronts and you will see the decayed flat façades of early-nineteenth-century houses. Farther along King's Road, the second opening on the left is the impressive Royal Avenue. Before turning into it, walk for another 100 yards along King's Road to where Markham Square opens on the right. The building at the corner of the square, no. 138 King's Road, now contains an unexciting-looking drugstore, but it was here that Mary Quant first went into business with a shop called Bazaar. When Quant, a young ex-student, and her backers converted the building into a shop, their enterprise was very nearly ruined at the outset. Planning permission for the architectural changes had not been obtained, and a local government official ordered Quant and her friends to restore the building to its original shape—at their own expense. The backers and Quant herself (in tears) besieged the official and in the end obtained the permission they wanted.

The shop began purely as a retail venture, with an associated restaurant in the basement. (Guests at the restaurant included Brigitte Bardot. When she appeared, service came to a standstill; the male waiters clustered around—to gaze at the beautiful man who accompanied her.) Mary Quant began designing when she found that she couldn't get from wholesalers the unusual designs she wanted. She later wrote a breathless and delightful book, *Quant by Quant*, about the chaotic but highly successful early days of her business. Many of her dress patterns were eaten by Siamese cats: "It took me some time to discover that the tissue paper used to make these patterns is manufactured from some by-product of fish bones." The name Bazaar was at the time zany and original, and the window displays were also meant to surprise. Once, when the theme was vacation clothes, the window was filled with milk bottles to suggest a hasty holiday departure. Mary Quant did her market research by listening se-

Window shopping, King's Road

Skinheads, King's Road

cretly to what passersby had to say about her displays through a ventilator in the shop wall.

Quant had more influence on the fashions of the sixties than perhaps anyone else in the world. Among her new ideas was the use for fashion of the shiny fabric polyvinylchloride. This became standard dress even for radicals who supposedly turned their backs on fashion. Many of the demonstrating anarchists and Marxists of the late sixties were, without knowing it, dressed for "battle" in the styles of Mary Quant.

Now go back along King's Road to Royal Avenue, a grand set of late Georgian terraces that face each other across lines of trees. Between the trees is a barren strip of stony land, too uneven for games and too rubbly for sitting on. The main users seem to be dogs. Walk along the right-hand side of the avenue, where you will see several fine old lights above the doors; look at the short, vertical metal bars set into the glass over the doors of nos. 14, 16 and 22. Near the far end, at no. 48, the second-story window has an extremely intricate set of wooden shutters behind it. Right at the end of the avenue, the road's original purpose becomes clear. By looking straight ahead, through the ornamental iron gates, you can see in the distance the Royal Hospital, built in the 1680s and 1690s as a home for soldiers. (A Latin inscription in the building says that it was designed for men "broken by war and old age.") Royal Avenue was meant to be part of a grand route joining the hospital and a palace at Kensington, but when its promoter, Charles II, died, the scheme was dropped.

By looking between the lines of trees that run towards the hospital, you can make out the cupola on its roof and also the rounded, baroque windows favored by its architect, Christopher Wren. Although still in use, the building has the feeling of a grand and rather bleak monument, and so it isn't on our route. (It can be visited in the afternoons, and if you'd like to be guided around the fine chapel and dining hall, one of the old soldiers will oblige eagerly. Payment is expected.) You may already have seen some of the building's residents wearing their uniform frock-coats and with the initials of the Royal Hospital on their caps. They are usually called "Chelsea pensioners": many have distinguished war records, and some have an envied ability to attract gifts of beer in local pubs. Nowadays almost all are elderly, but in earlier times younger men were admitted. In 1765 two of the pensioners attacked and murdered a traveler on the edge of Chelsea; evidently they weren't yet "broken by war and old age." They were caught and executed, and for months afterwards their tarred bodies hung twisting in the wind, as a macabre deterrent.

The road at the end of Royal Avenue is St. Leonard's

Terrace; turn left for a moment, and go along to the next corner on the left (Walpole Street). Here the smartly painted house, no. 7 St. Leonard's Terrace, was in the late 1970s the home of Laurence Olivier. In front of the house notice the artfully bulging railings of the balconies. Then retrace your steps along St. Leonard's Terrace back to Royal Avenue, and go about 100 yards farther. No. 18 St. Leonard's Terrace has a dignified plain frontage, with a metal canopy over the door and an ancient boot scraper outside it that dates from the days of muddy streets. Low railings with spikes prevent illegal access to the basement; their lowness leads you to guess that they were installed when people were, on average, a few inches shorter than they are today.

In the late nineteenth century this was the home of Bram Stoker, the tall and handsome Irish actor and novelist who invented Count Dracula. Stoker's novel *Dracula* was published in 1897, when he was living here. There was a historical Dracula, a certain Vlad Drakul who ruled Wallachia (now part of Rumania) in the fifteenth century and was famous for impaling his enemies on stakes. But it was Stoker who turned Dracula into a coffin-dwelling bloodsucker, with glamorous "undead" female followers. His Gothic novel, with its exaggerated horror and its interest in medieval ruins, shows signs of having been written in a great hurry. But it's still worth reading, especially the passage in which the count's young English victim, detained in Castle Dracula, first realizes that there is something very wrong about his host:

> The window at which I stood was tall and deep, stone mullioned, and though weather worn, was still complete;. . . I drew back behind the stonework, and looked carefully out.
>
> What I saw was the Count's head coming out from the window below. I did not see the face. . . . I was at first interested and somewhat amused . . . but my very feelings changed to repulsion and terror when I saw the whole man slowly emerge from the window and begin to crawl down the castle wall over that dreadful abyss, *face down,* with his cloak spread out around him like great wings. . . . I saw the fingers and toes grasp the corners of the stones, worn clear of the mortar by the stress of years,

Fruit barrow, Chelsea

and by thus using every projection and inequality move downwards with considerable speed, just as a lizard moves along a wall.

It is sad, perhaps, that Stoker himself did not realize the stage potential of his creation. The first serious stage production of *Dracula* was in 1924, twelve years after Stoker's death. When the show reached the West End, a nurse had to be employed to deal with the numerous people in the audience who fainted: seven was average for an evening; the maximum was twenty-nine. One report said of the people who fainted: "strangely enough, they were generally men." (All this made excellent publicity, and the show soon opened in New York with the leading role played by a little-known Hungarian who went on to become the definitive ghoul—Bela Lugosi. Lugosi also played in the superb 1931 Universal film *Dracula*. In the film, the monster at one point is climbing the stairs of his castle, passing through cobwebs which remain, of course, unbroken. Suddenly the howling of wolves is heard through a window—she-vampires calling to the Master. Dracula turns, his great cloak swirling around him, and his voice echoes down the stone staircase, "Listen to them—children of the night. What *music* they make.")

Next door to Stoker's house, at no. 19, the most beautiful section of St. Leonard's Terrace begins. Creeping plants reach high up the fronts of the elegant eighteenth-century houses, which look out over fields towards the Royal Hospital. At no. 20 notice how the low garden wall has developed a bulge over the years. Between nos. 21 and 22 are delicate iron railings. Nos. 26–30 are the oldest houses in the row, dating from the mid-eighteenth century. No. 26 has an intricately carved wooden doorframe, like its neighbors. Above the door is a light with strips of metal that intersect to form pointed, Gothic arches.

Just beyond these houses, at the intersection with Smith Street, is a mailbox ("pillar box") from Stoker's day. It is about five feet high, hexagonal in design and has a petal motif on the top. It bears the insignia of Queen Victoria (VR—Victoria Regina). Above the narrow slit for letters is the royal badge of lion and uni-

Victorian mailbox, St. Leonard's Terrace

corn. Today Victorian pillar boxes of this type are rare survivors. In most areas they have long been removed, probably because of the narrowness of the slit. But in Chelsea style is more likely to be put before convenience, and the residents are powerful enough to have their views respected by the Post Office.

Turn right, into Smith Street, for a moment. Thirty yards along, on the left, is the entry to Smith Terrace, a delightful crescent of small Georgian houses. Originally built for fairly humble residents, the terrace has now been revamped and painted in pastel shades. Opposite nos. 3–5 of the terrace sits a grim contrast—a dingy and decayed commercial building with broken windows. In faded paint on the side it is announced that this once housed engineers "by appointment to His Majesty the King." It's not clear which king is meant, but by the age of the lettering I would guess George V (1910–36). This building isn't only hideous; it's also tall enough to overshadow the pretty houses across the street. No doubt the neighbors love it.

Go back to Smith Street and turn right. There will now be a walk of a few hundred yards which will bring you into Old Chelsea's most bohemian quarter. Return to the corner with the Victorian pillar box, and carry on straight ahead, passing a terrace on the right called Durham Place and then its continuation, Ormonde Gate. Where this street ends—at the junction with Royal Hospital Road—turn right and then into the first street on the left, Tite Street. This street has far more history, and chic, than its rather ordinary-looking buildings and empty sidewalks might suggest. On the right of the street is a tall terrace of red brick Victorian houses with balconies and bow fronts. Here at no. 34 (formerly no. 16) was the home of Oscar Wilde.

Wilde, a young playwright from Dublin, moved here shortly after his marriage, in 1884, to Constance Lloyd, "a beautiful girl" (in Wilde's words), "a grave, slight, violet-eyed little Artemis, with great coils of heavy brown hair which make her flower-like head droop like a blossom." They had two children soon afterwards. Helped by Constance's money, Wilde turned the interior of the house into an aesthete's paradise. The room just to the right of the front door was a study, with walls of buttercup yellow set off with red lacquer. The dining room was decorated in shades of white, with "each table a sonnet in ivory, and the main table . . . a masterpiece in pearl." Wilde's house was to be "a tower of ivory," with unpleasantness utterly excluded.

By the 1890s Wilde's plays were earning him a great deal of money, and he spent much of it on boys and young men, among them Lord Alfred Douglas. In 1895 unpleasantness arrived here at Wilde's door, in the shape of Douglas's father, the Marquess of Queensberry. Queensberry, a member of a famous sporting family, was appalled by his son's homosexual behavior and had come to remonstrate with Wilde. He was, however, firmly invited to leave, with Wilde telling his servant, so that the Marquess could hear, never again to let in "the most infamous brute in London." Queensberry retaliated by going to Wilde's club and leaving a note addressed to "Oscar Wilde posing as a somdomite" (a misspelling which consequently became famous). Wilde was greatly upset, exclaiming that "the tower of ivory is assailed by the foul thing." He prosecuted the Marquess for libel, lost, and caused so much evidence to emerge that he himself became liable for prosecution as a homosexual. The police gave him time to flee the country, perhaps following orders from on high (Wilde had some important political connections). But instead he sat drinking with Lord Alfred Douglas until he was arrested. He was given two years' imprisonment, and later wrote *The Ballad of Reading Gaol* about his experiences. Popular with prisoners and warders, he used to help the warders prepare their entries for newspaper literary competitions. The staff of Reading prison suddenly found themselves winning substantial prizes, including a tea service and a grand piano.

Even after his disgrace, some of Wilde's work remained popular. His play *The Importance of Being Earnest* kept on running (though with the author's name removed from all the advertisements). For this play Wilde invented an upper-class monster, Lady Bracknell, a character still well remembered in England. When a young man wishes to marry her daughter, Lady Bracknell questions him about his social origins and respectability, and explodes on being told that he doesn't know his origins because he was found as a baby in a handbag in a station cloakroom. She informs the young man that discovery in a handbag can hardly be regarded as a secure basis for a career in society, adding "You can hardly imagine that I and Lord Bracknell would dream of allowing our only daughter—a girl brought up with the utmost care—to marry into a cloakroom, and form an alliance with a parcel."

Wilde is master of the shrewd and memorable overstatement: "Work is the curse of the drinking classes," "Men become old but they never become good," "The very essence of romance is uncertainty" and "Hard work is simply the refuge of people who have nothing whatever to do." Even during his trial he found time to make phrases: "All is well," he said; "the working classes are with me—to a boy."

Soon after Wilde's imprisonment, Queensberry arranged to have him driven into bankruptcy. The contents of "the house beautiful" here were virtually looted and Wilde's wife and children were driven out. Wilde suffered, after his release, as an impoverished exile. In different ways, so did his wife. One of their young sons summed up the position well, towards the end of their stay in Tite Street. Wilde had scolded him for being a naughty boy and for making mother cry; the young Wilde replied that Oscar was a "naughty Papa," who "did not come home till the early morning and made mother cry far more."

A few yards farther down Tite Street, on the left, is a small irregular block with very large windows. It contained studios in Chelsea's artistic heyday. In the first section (no. 31) John Singer Sargent worked for many years; he eventually died here in 1925. American by parentage and European by upbringing, Sargent produced many imposing oil paintings of wealthy young women, usually wearing extravagantly beautiful dresses. He may have performed the role of earlier portraitists in the days before photography—helping to attract suitable husbands for young ladies with dowries. Highly successful in its day, Sargent's work is still respected on both sides of the Atlantic.

Next door, at no. 33, the Welsh portraitist Augustus John had a studio in the years around 1950. A charismatic figure, bearded and with loose-fitting clothes,

John attracted and occasionally mistreated numerous women. Among his best-remembered works today is a sketch of T. E. Lawrence in Arab headdress, looking spiritual and decisive.

Just beyond this block, on the same side of the street, is a white, modern house (no. 35) with walls covered by concrete slabs. Until the late 1970s this belonged to a gentleman named the Honorable Colin Tennant, the owner of the Caribbean holiday island of Mustique. Among his guests on the island have been Princess Margaret and her friend Roddy Llewellyn. When Tennant decided to sell this house, it was advertised at £500,000. A few weeks later, I was pointing out the place to some friends when a grand Chelsea lady came past. "That," she informed us, "has just been sold to the Arabs for half a million pounds," and swept away. Notice: the Arabs. People in West London, where many Arabs have recently bought houses, often get conspiracy-minded.

A more famous house once stood on this site, the "white house" built in the 1870s for the admired American painter James McNeill Whistler, by the architect E. W. Godwin. Whistler loved Chelsea and produced many impressionistic paintings of the Thames in this area. His house in Tite Street, built of white brick and green slate, was to be home, studio and school. But while the house was being built, a painting of Whistler's—*The Falling Rocket, a Nocturne in Black and Gold*—was attacked in print by the art critic John Ruskin. Ruskin, objecting to the impressionism and lack of precise detail, claimed that Whistler was impudently asking 200 guineas (£210) for "flinging a pot of paint in the public's face." Whistler sued for libel, won his case, was awarded one farthing—a quarter of a penny—in damages and ordered to pay his own enormous legal costs. He was, temporarily, ruined. He tried to persuade creditors to accept his own paintings instead of cash (which, as it turned out, would have been a wonderful bargain), but the offer was rejected. One creditor wrote back, "It is not a Nocturne in purple or a Symphony in blue and grey that we are after, but an Arrangement in gold and silver." Whistler was forced to sell his beloved house in 1879 before it was completed. Just before leaving, he wrote above the front door, "Except the Lord build the house, they labour in vain that build it. E. W. Godwin built this one."

Opposite the modern white house is the start of Dilke Street. Go along here for a few steps, then turn for a moment into the first opening on the right, Paradise Walk. After an unpromising first section, this is now a prettily painted terrace of two-storied Georgian cottages with wooden shutters outside the windows. But in the mid-nineteenth century it was one of London's worst slums, its houses packed with ragged families. Oscar Wilde's "tower of ivory" overlooked the back of this street; he put a screen over his window to block the view.

Come back to Dilke Street, turn right and, a few yards farther, look into the next entrance on the right, Clover Mews. (A mews is a terrace, with residential quarters above a first story which was once stables and is now converted into garages. The word *mews* came from the French *muer*, "to molt," and originally meant a place where tame hawks were kept during their periods of molting. The residential part of a mews is usually small, as here.) It might seem strange that the blank, imposing garage doors have not been removed and the space behind them converted into living accommodations. The explanation is that such conversion would destroy the street's character as a mews and spoil the owners' investment; mews properties are fashionable and expensive. Notice the flagstones in the street outside, which add to the antique atmosphere, and the window boxes—de rigueur for mews-dwellers.

Turn right into Dilke Street again. A few steps farther and you will come to the end of the street. The road which runs left and right here is Swan Walk, one of the most pleasant of Chelsea's quiet places. The name Swan came from the (now vanished) Swan Inn, which stood on the old river bank close to where you're standing. The river was pushed back to its present banks when the Chelsea Embankment was built in the early 1870s. Samuel Pepys describes paying a visit to this spot at the time of the Great Plague, and getting a shock:

> By coach to Mrs. Pierce's and with her and (Mrs.) Knipp and Mrs. Pierce's boy and girl abroad, thinking to have

been merry at Chelsea; but being come almost to the house by coach near the waterside, a house alone, I think the Swan, a gentleman walking by called to us to tell us that the house was shut up of the sickness. So we with great affright turned back ... and went away (I for my part in great disorder).

Pepys mentions how grateful he felt to this gentleman for preventing them from going any closer to the place of infection.

Facing you, on the far side of Swan Walk, is a long wall about eight feet high. Behind it is the private Physic Garden: go 50 yards to the right along Swan Walk and you can look in through an iron gate. The garden was first laid out in the 1670s by the apothecaries—herbalists who played an important role in English medicine. Here their precious plants grew; notice on top of the gate the wicked old spikes to prevent intruders. In 1685 the diarist John Evelyn visited the garden, described the ingenious system of underground heating in the plant-houses and noted the tree that produced Jesuits' bark, "which had done such cures in quartans." (Quartan ague was malaria, and Jesuits' bark contained quinine.) Later, in 1722, the apothecaries ran into financial difficulties, and Sir Hans Sloane generously leased them the garden at a fixed low rent. In recognition, they set up a marble statue of Sloane, made by a leading sculptor of the 1730s, Michael Rysbrack. You can see it straight ahead of you through the gate; Sloane is wearing a full-bottomed wig.

In 1732 the garden provided help for a new colony in America, designed for poor debtors and named Georgia after the British monarch of the day, George II. A supply of cottonseed was sent from here to Georgia, and from that seed developed the great cotton industry of the American South. Years later, Britain in turn came to rely on imports of cotton from America. During the American Civil War, the blockade of the southern states prevented this cotton from reaching England, with dire results. About a fifth of the English population depended on the cotton industry, and pressure was put on the British government to join the war on the side of the Confederates—which it nearly did. In those days, British naval intervention mattered; the British navy was the largest in the world, and less than fifty years had passed since a British force had won the battle of Bladensburg and burned Washington. However, in 1861 Queen Victoria's husband, Prince Albert, intervened from his deathbed to prevent the British government from sending an inflammatory message to the Union government. If sent, this would probably have brought Britain into the war, and might perhaps have altered its result. So the cottonseeds from this garden had some far-reaching effects.

Also in the 1730s the Physic Garden was used by one of the greatest of botanical artists, Elizabeth Blackwell. Until her day, accurate illustrations of herbs were difficult or impossible to find. She made herself an expert through years of studying the plants in this garden, and produced a meticulous and beautifully illustrated book entitled *A Curious* (careful) *Herbal*. Part of her long task was to color the printed illustrations by hand. Copies of the book still exist, and under each illustration is written in Latin, "Elizabeth Blackwell drew, engraved and painted this." The text, compiled by her husband, was less original, but has some interesting entries: "Turnips are accounted very wholesome and nourishing, but somewhat windy. A syrup, made with slices of turnip and brown sugar candy baked in an oven, is commended as a good pectoral, and of great service for coughs and consumptions." Some of Mrs. Blackwell's illustrations show insects associated with the plants. With the garden radish is shown the "Mole Cricket—It lives commonly upon roots, and seldom comes abroad till ye sun is down."

It seems that Elizabeth Blackwell produced this book to help herself and her husband out of serious debt caused by his failure as a printer. While doing her research, she lived in Swan Walk, probably at no. 4. (The building is still standing, a fine detached Georgian house just across the road.) Mr. Blackwell, however, got into further trouble. He went to work at the court of Sweden, became suspected of plotting and was sentenced to death. An English newspaper of the time reported that when Blackwell knelt at the block, the executioner told him that he was on the wrong side of it. He replied dryly that the mistake was under-

Strollers, Chelsea

standable, since this was the first time he had ever been beheaded. Elizabeth Blackwell survived her husband, and was buried in Chelsea Old Church in 1758.

Behind their railings and garden walls, the detached eighteenth-century houses in Swan Walk are three-storied and of faded brick. At no. 2, notice the hanging-basket design of the ancient oil lamp over the gate, and the fine Corinthian columns of the door frame (best seen from the far side of the road).

Just beyond no. 1 Swan Walk is Royal Hospital Road again. Turn left into it, and walk the 150 yards to the junction with Flood Street (on the right). Flood Street itself isn't on the present route, but at the far end of it—no. 19—is the family home of Mrs. Margaret Thatcher. The house, prosperous and unexciting in appearance, is guarded by one of the very few British policemen to carry a gun as a matter of course.

Also joining Royal Hospital Road here, and forming a corner with Flood Street, is Cheyne Walk, one of London's most chic addresses. It is a single line of houses, built to look out over the river and now sheltered from the traffic of Chelsea Embankment by a strip of small trees. The brickwork of the flat, elegant, housefronts has mellowed over the years, and most of the older houses have had a story or two added, but otherwise they remain much as they were built, which was just before 1720, early in the Georgian era. For over a century Cheyne Walk has been the home of people successful in the arts and show business.

A few yards along the walk, at no. 3, you can see the wooden shutters behind the first-story windows. In the early 1970s this was the home of Keith Richards, the Rolling Stones guitarist, songwriter and pharmaceutical expert. When the Stones first became known in the early sixties, their manager, Andrew Loog Oldham, tried to publicize mildly unpleasant aspects of the group to give it a distinct image. The Beatles at the time were being sold as cuddly lads from the homely north of England, the sort that any grandmother would be happy to have visiting her teenage granddaughter. So the Stones had to appear as nasties from the decadent English south.

Next door, no. 4 has plants creeping above the tall iron gateway. Look up at the date molded into the head of the drainpipe: 1718. In the 1860s this was the

home of Daniel Maclise, an Irish artist. He was a drinking companion of Charles Dickens, and produced both flattering and satirical portraits of him.

Later, in 1880, this was the home for a few weeks of Mary Ann Evans (George Eliot), one of the cleverest—and, to some, one of the most notorious—women of Victorian England. Educated in the unfashionable Midland city of Coventry, she moved to London for work and companionship and became the brains behind an intellectual magazine, the *Westminster Review*. When she began to write fiction, she was extremely nervous about criticism. Even her publisher was not allowed to know her identity, and she chose a male nom de plume to defeat guesswork. She revealed her secret after her work had proved an immediate success and someone in the Midlands had begun to claim that *he* was George Eliot.

George Eliot took pride in the sympathetic but exact description of motives. Especially close to her heart were the characters of Dorothea Brooke and Maggie Tulliver, the young heroines of *Middlemarch* and *The Mill on the Floss*. Dorothea is willing to give away much of her time and fortune to help the poor, but guiltily catches herself wishing that there were slightly more poverty in the neighborhood for her to remedy.

Maggie Tulliver as a child is frowned on by her mother for being dark-haired and lively, not blonde and docile like a fashionable girl. But Maggie has her own views about this. She decides to cut off her offending hair, thinking "of the triumph she should have over her mother and her aunts by this very decided course of action: she didn't want her hair to look pretty—that was out of the question—she only wanted people to think her a clever little girl, and not to find fault with her." Her mother despairs of this wayward daughter, but her father has a gleam of hope: perhaps she will grow up clever enough to defeat the local lawyers.

Eliot's feminism is gently acidic, directed against male conceit, against occasionally silly women and also against the men who encourage them to be so. When a woman in *The Mill on the Floss* says something unusually stupid, her husband smiles happily "with the natural pride of a man who has a buxom wife conspicuously his inferior in intellect." The shallow Sir James Chettam, who tries to court Dorothea in *Middlemarch*, feels himself quite unthreatened by her superior brains. He, after all, is a man, and "a man's mind—what there is of it—has always the advantage of being masculine, as the smallest birch-tree is of a higher kind than the most soaring palm, and even his ignorance is of a sounder quality."

For much of her life, Eliot created scandal by living with the biographer George Lewes. She would have liked to marry him, and she called herself Mrs. Lewes. Lewes, however, was already married. He had treated his wife well, continuing to support her after she had begun to have children by another man, which was before George Eliot came on the scene. But by thus condoning his wife's adultery he had made divorce impossible. Unlike some Victorians, Queen Victoria herself was not put off Eliot's work by the scandal; she was said to be devoted to the novels and eagerly acquired the writer's autograph.

Lewes died in 1878. In the spring of 1880 Eliot married John Cross, a banker more than twenty years her junior. During their honeymoon in Venice, Cross—in a fit of depression—jumped out of a window into a canal. He was pulled out alive, and recovered slowly. He and his wife moved into this house on December 3, 1880. On December 19 she fell ill, and died three days later. Cross wrote, "And I am left alone in this new house we meant to be so happy in."

Next door, no. 5 Cheyne Walk is now smartly painted and was until recently the home of a Duchess of Devonshire, one of the wealthy Cavendish family. But in the nineteenth century this was the dingy, cobwebbed home of a miser named Neild. Having inherited a fortune from his father, a jeweler, Neild spent much of his life trudging the roads collecting rents from his numerous properties. When he died in 1852 he left half a million pounds—then a colossal fortune—to Queen Victoria. Critics said that his surviving relatives deserved the money more, but Victoria accepted it.

No. 6, adjoining, has only four floors, and shows more clearly than its neighbors how Cheyne Walk looked when first built. The front is brick of various colors. Notice, too, the large, crumbling wooden gates, the worn stone steps bonded with iron and the iron-studded door to the basement (on the right). On the wall above the main door are two metal firemarks; a resident around 1800 was unusually afraid of losing his property, and insured with two fire brigades at once. One mark has the clasped hands of the Amicable Contributors company; the other, showing a lion in a circle, belongs to the British Fire Office. Occasionally a building from this period had even more firemarks; and it was said of King George IV, who liked to decorate himself with numerous medals, that he "looked like an over-insured building." Look at the top of the meandering drainpipes, and you will see the coat of arms of the first residents here in the early eighteenth century, the Danvers family, gentry from the Midlands. When the family left, the place was taken, in 1765, by a Dr. Dominiceti, a Venetian who aimed to cure wealthy patients with vapor baths. After spending huge sums to convert the interior into bath chambers, Dominiceti found his patients falling away and his debts mounting. He left England, and his creditors, in a hurry.

A few doors along, no. 10 Cheyne Walk was the home in the 1970s of an artistic couple, well known in Britain: Jane Asher and Gerald Scarfe. Asher is an actress with a successful record on the West End stage. In the 1960s she became famous as a girl friend of Paul

McCartney. Asher looked like an angel, McCartney looked like a choirboy—the nation approved the match, except for McCartney's female fans, of course. Asher also won hearts during a television broadcast when a large spider entered the studio and approached her, unscripted. The gentle-looking lady did not retreat, but picked the spider up sympathetically and removed it. Gerald Scarfe is a successful cartoonist, his political work appearing weekly in the *Sunday Times*. He made his name in the sixties, producing venomously distorted caricatures for the satirical magazine *Private Eye*. He has a particular liking for anti-Kremlin cartoons. In 1968, at the time of the Russian invasion of Czechoslovakia and also of the first heart-transplant operations, Scarfe did a cartoon showing Brezhnev and Kosygin, dressed as surgeons, operating on a familiar figure from the Russian past. "Stalin," the caption read, "—New Heart."

Go along to no. 16 Cheyne Walk, a Georgian house which in 1862 became the home of Dante Gabriel Rossetti. Rossetti belonged to the Pre-Raphaelite group of painters who tried to bring back the intense and detailed style used in early Italian art. He was also a successful poet. When he moved here, Rossetti was recovering from the death of his wife, the beautiful Elizabeth Siddal. He had met her when she was a hat-maker's assistant. She suffered from tuberculosis, but sat for many of Rossetti's paintings and was also the subject of several of his love poems. (Many Victorians liked their women "pale and interesting," as Thomas Hardy put it.) The illness was well advanced when she married Rossetti, and she "seemed ready to die daily." When she did die, the distraught and romantic Rossetti had some of his love poems buried with her, wrapped in her lovely hair. Seven years later, when his love for her had dwindled but the value of the poems had not, he made the less romantic gesture of having her dug up to get the manuscripts back. Luckily, she—and they—were quite well preserved.

In this house and its back garden Rossetti kept exotic animals, imported at great expense. Two kangaroos (mother and son) lived in a shed until the young

one committed matricide. Later this naughty animal was itself killed, probably by Rossetti's pet raccoon. The artist was especially fond of his wombat, a cuddly Australian marsupial that looks like a large dormouse. Lewis Carroll (Charles Dodgson) visited Rossetti here, and it is thought that the wombat was the original model of the dormouse in the Mad Hatter's Tea Party. One lady who was sitting for a portrait by Rossetti had her straw hat eaten by the wombat. Rossetti was most sympathetic—to the animal: "Ah, poor wombat. It is so indigestible." Most anarchic of all were Rossetti's armadillos, which used to burrow under walls and emerge triumphantly in the neighboring gardens. In a particularly successful breakout, one armadillo dug its way up through a neighbor's kitchen floor, terrifying the cook.

Above the gate of no. 16, half hidden in the decorative ironwork, are the initials of its first resident, Richard Chapman, an apothecary, who leased the place in 1717. A recent resident was Mr. Paul Getty, and you may still see a closed-circuit TV camera by the door. Just across the road, behind the hedge in the public garden, is a bust of Rossetti set up by his friends. He is shown with palette and writing paper to hint at his double artistic role. A plaque on one side says "Born 1828"; the corresponding plaque for his death (in 1882) has been removed by a vandal.

When you are a few yards farther along Cheyne Walk, go down the alley (Cheyne Mews) that opens to the right and passes close to the front door (and fine fanlight) of no. 24. An ancient sign tells you that "This road is reserved for residents and their horses and vehicles." A brief inspection is allowable all the same. The alley passes through a tunnel below no. 24, where there is another sign for those with vehicles: "All drivers of Vehicles are Directed to *Walk* their Horses while passing under this Archway."

Go 60 yards farther down this lane, which is almost as quiet as the country. At the end is a cluster of mews cottages. This was the site of Henry VIII's manor house until its demolition in 1753. Henry gave the house to his last Queen, Catherine Parr, upon their marriage in 1543. The King was by this time exceedingly fat; his surviving fourth wife, Anne of Cleves, who also lived

here for a time, said with understandable spite that she did not envy the new Queen her "heavy burden." Catherine continued her residence after Henry's death four years later, and was soon being courted by the ambitious Thomas Seymour, Lord High Admiral. She sent him instructions on how to visit her secretly in the garden here very early in the morning. After marrying Catherine, however, Seymour showed an eye for further flirtation with royalty. The young Princess Elizabeth was also living here. Seymour used to enter her bedroom in his nightshirt and try to kiss and cuddle her. Catherine had Elizabeth removed, amid scandalous gossip: the future Virgin Queen angrily denied a rumor that she had been imprisoned in the Tower of London, "with child by the Lord Admiral."

Seymour was beheaded soon afterwards, but the most tragic of all the Tudor residents was Jane Grey, daughter of the Duke of Suffolk and great-granddaughter of King Henry VII. At the age of nine, she came to live here for a time with Queen Catherine. Cruelly treated by her parents, she got more kindness from her tutor and responded by becoming an excellent student. By the age of thirteen she was known in England and abroad for her ability to speak as well as write Classical Greek. A visitor to her family home in Leicestershire found her reading Plato while the rest of her family was out hunting.

At fifteen she was forced to make a political marriage with Guildford Dudley, son of the powerful Duke of Northumberland. She had at first refused to marry him, but her father beat her into submission. When Henry VIII's son Edward VI died in 1553, Jane was put forward as Queen by her scheming relatives, and "reigned" for nine days before being overcome by the forces of Henry's daughter, Mary. Under sentence of death, at the age of sixteen, Jane was calm and impressive. From a window in the Tower of London she watched her husband taken off in procession, and a few minutes later saw his headless corpse brought back. Later the same day she went to the scaffold herself. Blindfolded, she was left to grope helplessly for the block, asking "Where is it? What should I do?" A tall executioner dressed in scarlet took off her head. Back in Leicestershire the family servants are said to have cut off the tops of the oak trees as a memorial to their talented and brave Queen Jane.

Come back into Cheyne Walk and turn right. Just ahead is the noisy junction of Chelsea Embankment and Oakley Street. As you approach it, look at no. 27 Cheyne Walk, on the right. This was Bram Stoker's home in the early 1880s, until he was persuaded to leave it by his wife, who had had a frightening experience here. Stoker, while traveling on a Thames steamboat, had seen an old man climb the rails and drop into the river. Although a rapid and dangerous tide was running, Stoker went in, caught him and swam with him back to the boat. He then arranged for the man to be brought to this house. He was, however, found to be dead, and after having the corpse in her dining room Mrs. Stoker took a permanent disliking to the place.

Crossing the Thames at this point is the Albert Bridge, built in 1873, a masterpiece of ornate Victorian ironwork, using both cantilever and suspension principles. Until recently a notice at the end of the bridge told parties of soldiers to break step while crossing. (Even a massive and soundly built bridge can be brought down by the vibrations of a group of people marching in step.)

Cross Oakley Street to where Cheyne Walk continues, close to a piece of modern sculpture showing a boy and dolphin. Farther along, at no. 48 Cheyne Walk, the thick stems of creeping plants have twisted tightly around the metal supports of a balcony. In the early 1970s this was Mick Jagger's house. Just beyond is the junction of Cheyne Walk and Cheyne Row. The pub on the far corner, The King's Head and Eight Bells, is fashionable and very good for lunches. Notice the modern copper-framed gaslights outside. Turn into Cheyne Row and 50 yards along on the right is a plaque from the time its oldest houses were built; it's set into the side wall of no. 16, about 20 feet up, and reads "This is Cheyne Row, 1708." Above the front door of no. 18, and best seen from across the street, is a delicately painted fire mark with the policy number of some long-dead insurer. At no. 24 (formerly no. 5) is the house of Thomas Carlyle, a biographer and historian revered in his time but now largely forgotten. Carlyle lived here—in what was already an old house—from 1834 until his death in 1881. The house is kept as a museum, as we shall see in a moment. In his work, Carlyle claimed that nations ought to submit to the rule of gifted and heroic leaders, an idea with dangers that are obvious nowadays. (His special admiration for Frederick the Great of Prussia was shared, many years later, by Hitler.) But in private life Carlyle could be extraordinarily generous. As a young writer, he gave much of his small and insecure income to help in his brother's education. And when the philosopher John Stuart Mill lost the only copy of a work that had taken Carlyle months to produce, the author's main concern was to prevent Mill from finding out how much damage he had done.

The house is open from April to October, and a guided tour is given for a small fee. When you ring for admission, you will hear the eighteenth-century bell sounding inside. The interior is almost exactly as it was in Carlyle's day. His hat still hangs in the hall, though now it is discreetly secured to its peg to foil souvenir hunters. On the walls there is full-length wooden paneling: Carlyle was very excited about this; his wife less so. She thought of the bugs that might be living securely behind it.

In the front basement is a fine kitchen with a stone floor. For many years water was pumped from a well below. The kitchen range is a delight of economy; the open fireplace could be regulated to fit different size fires by the movement of one side, and the fire itself heated both a water tank and an oven. Carlyle's woman servant slept in the kitchen; in common Victorian style, she wasn't allowed her own bedroom. Upstairs you will see the four-poster that Mrs. Carlyle brought here (she herself had been born in it). On a windowpane there's a clearly legible bit of graffiti, scratched by a young window cleaner in the 1790s.

Go a few steps farther up Cheyne Row to the first crossroad, Upper Cheyne Row, which runs to the left and right. This meeting place of eighteenth-century streets is one of the quietest corners in Chelsea. The narrow entrance to Upper Cheyne Row on the left was designed to let through a single horse-drawn carriage. The iron posts standing near the edge of the sidewalk were to prevent carriages from cutting corners (literally) and endangering pedestrians. Several of the small Georgian houses have pleasant and distinctive lights above their doors; look at nos. 30, 24 and 22.

Turn for a moment into the section of Upper Cheyne Row on the right. The fifth house along, no. 22, was in the 1830s the home of Leigh Hunt, a radical journalist and friend of the poets Shelley, Byron and Keats. Hunt had become famous in 1812 when he clashed with the Prince Regent (later King George IV). A conservative newspaper had stated that the Prince was an "Adonis of loveliness, attended by pleasure, honour, virtue and truth." The reality, however, was rather different. Leigh Hunt and his brother, carried away by love of truth, printed a reply in their own newspaper:

> This Adonis in Loveliness was a corpulent man of fifty. . . . This delightful, blissful, wise, honourable, virtuous, true and immortal prince was a violator of his word, a libertine over head and ears in disgrace, a despiser of domestic ties; the companion of gamblers and demireps [demimondaines], a man who has just closed half a century without one single claim on the gratitude of his country . . .

For this the brothers were sentenced to two years' imprisonment and ordered to pay large fines—unless they promised not to attack the Prince again. They refused, and made themselves minor heroes by going to prison instead. Georgian prisons, though often appalling and disease-ridden places, were in some ways far more liberal than those of today. To make his own cell bearable, Leigh Hunt had roses painted on the walls and a sky scene on the ceiling. He was allowed books and a piano. His wife and famous writers paid him visits.

A few years later, in 1820, Hunt had the satisfaction of seeing his words justified and his royal enemy truly "over head and ears in disgrace." By now George was King and his estranged second wife, Caroline of Brunswick, was in name the Queen of England. In 1820 he tried to divorce her, almost causing a revolution. Troops mutinied, loyalist politicians were mobbed and large groups of demure and respected citizens demonstrated in support of Caroline. Before the House of Lords George's representatives tried to prove that the Queen had had an affair with a handsome Italian gentleman named Bergami. She almost certainly had, but the King himself was famous for his mistresses and the royal accusation of adultery seemed hopelessly hypocritical. One Italian witness, summoned to help the King's case, lost his nerve when confronted with the pomp of the House of Lords and replied in answer to over fifty questions, *"non mi ricordo"* ("I don't remember"). Caroline's supporters were triumphant, and banners waved in London with *"non mi ricordo"* gleefully inscribed. (If you visit the National Portrait

Gallery, near Trafalgar Square, look for the large painting of Caroline's "trial" before the Lords. Beside it is displayed a yellowing contemporary copy of a *"non mi ricordo"* poem.) George's case eventually collapsed, perhaps because Caroline's lawyer threatened to reveal that the King was a bigamist. Caroline died in 1821, a few days after being physically shut out of George's Coronation at Westminster Abbey.

By the 1830s Leigh Hunt had fallen on hard times. While living here he was often unable to buy bread. Carlyle, who had known severe poverty himself, wrote rather callously of the squalor in Hunt's home:

> Hunt's house excels all you have ever read of—a pocket tinkerdom, without parallel even in literature. In his family room, where are a sickly large wife and a whole school of well-conditioned wild children, you will find half-a-dozen old rickety chairs gathered from half-a-dozen different hucksters. . . . On these and around them and over the dusty table and carpet lie all kinds of litter—books, papers, egg-shells, scissors, and last night, when I was there, the torn heart of a loaf. . . .

Like other bold people of the Georgian era, Hunt mellowed with the coming of the Victorian age. He escaped poverty in 1840 by writing a successful romantic play.

Go back to the crossroads and go through the narrow carriageway straight ahead of you. A few yards farther on, where this road opens into Lawrence Street, is a fine row of tiny cottages on the left. On one of them, no. 19, is a portrait of Queen Anne, in whose reign they were built. (She was the last Stuart monarch, and died in 1714.) Across the road, no. 15 Lawrence Street is the site of a mid-eighteenth-century pottery, where expensive figures were made in the pastoral style fashionable in France before the revolution. China shepherdesses toyed with pet lambs, and were courted by elegant, leisured shepherds. The factory has now entirely disappeared; its site was rediscovered only in 1970, when innumerable china fragments were unearthed in the garden of no. 15. Several products of the factory have survived and are now highly valued. Thea Holme, in her interesting book on Chelsea, tells of the owner of one china piece who de-

Artist's studio, Lawrence Street

cided in 1929 to auction it, hoping to raise £100 to buy a used car. Instead the object fetched £3,250, enough at the time to buy several houses.

When you are a little farther along Lawrence Street, turn right for a moment into the narrow Justice Walk to look at the magnificently carved doorcase of no. 6, 20 yards down on the right. Then come back to Lawrence Street, turn right, and at no. 11 you will see the tall and elegant bow window of an artist's studio, supported by carved brackets. It's best viewed from across the street, from where you will also see the miniature oval window above it.

A few steps farther down Lawrence Street is a pub, The Cross Keys. Inside there is much pleasant old woodwork and in winter an open fire. Good pub lunches are served and also Real Ale (ask for Director's). Tucked away in this quiet street, the place isn't often found by passersby. Instead, it is sought out by knowing customers, who sometimes come from quite a distance and can be quite possessive about "their" pub.

Just beyond the pub, Lawrence Street joins Cheyne Walk. The apartment block on the left corner here, Carlyle Mansions, is where the novelist Henry James died in 1916. Turn right into Cheyne Walk and straight ahead you will see Chelsea Old Church. Most of this small building was bombed to bits in 1941 by a land mine probably meant for one of the large power stations nearby. Luckily, the section where least damage was done was the one built in Henry VIII's time by Thomas More.

As you reach the church, you can see an ornate tomb with an urn beneath a canopy of stone. This is the burial place of Hans Sloane, physician and local landlord. Around the urn are carved snakes, symbols of Asclepius, the Greek god of healing. More's chapel is in the corner of the church just behind this tomb. Go along to the left of the church, passing an unfortunate modern statue of More. More is shown dressed almost entirely in somber black but with a golden face; the bulky statue sits looking out towards the river and resembles an elephantine version of a cheap icon.

Go to the end of the church wall, turn right, and you will find the entrance to the church. If you go in, look for the dark slab set into the wall just to the right

of the main altar. This is More's epitaph, in Latin and drafted by More himself some time before his support of the papacy against Henry VIII brought him to the block. The first two words of line one are his name in

Latin, *"Thomas Morus."* Now look fifteen lines down where, near the beginning of the line, there's a famous gap. The text reads, *"furibus autem et homicidis—* [blank] *molestus,"* meaning that More was "to thieves, however, and murderers—[blank] an oppressor." Where the blank now stands, More originally intended to write *"et hereticis,"* claiming that he was a persecutor also of heretics. According to the story, he was dissuaded from this boast by the kindly Dutch scholar Erasmus. Although impressive in several ways, More was not quite the gentle, lovable figure portrayed in the film *A Man for All Seasons.* He approved warmly of the execution of humble people for holding unorthodox religious views. Above the stone arch over More's epitaph is the dark face of a Moor, an African. Heraldic devices often involved a pun on the owner's name.

Turn left as you walk away from the altar and go into the little chapel that More built. Here on the wall a brass plate from the 1550s records the burial of Jane Guildford. By the time she died, her husband (the Duke of Northumberland), her son and her daughter-in-law (Jane Grey) had all been executed. A few inches to the right of her epitaph a superb, multicolored brass plate shows a Tudor lady at prayer.

A little farther along the same side of the church are the large alabaster effigies of two grandly named Elizabethan aristocrats, Lord and Lady Dacre of the South. Their effigies lie side by side: she wears the ruff fashionable at the time and he wears armor. His helmet, not an alabaster copy but the original, hangs above the tomb, a little to the right. Notice, too, that beside his effigy is an alabaster model of a dead infant daughter.

To end the walk, you may like to go along the pleasant Old Church Street—the road leading to the right as you leave the church door. In a few hundred yards this will bring you to one of the liveliest parts of the King's Road.

Restaurants, Shops
and Pubs

Restaurants

COVENT GARDEN

Tango, 37 Long Acre, WC2, tel. 836-7639. Argentinian recipes; the empanadas (meat in pastry) are especially recommended. Portions rather small, but always an elegant insufficiency. Inexpensive, spacious and with style.

Simeoni's, 43 Drury Lane, WC2, tel. 836-8296. Well-cooked, moderately priced Italian food.

Tutton's, 11 Russell Street, WC2, tel. 836-1167. Cheerful and crowded at midday and evening. Waitresses penetrate the crush with marvelous efficiency. Youngish clientele; food a good value and inexpensive.

Porter's, 17 Henrietta Street, WC2, tel. 836-6466. A creditable imitation of Tutton's, specializing in pies.

Rule's, 35 Maiden Lane, WC2, tel. 836-5314. Fairly expensive and sedate, with fine Victorian furnishings. Traditional English as well as French recipes. Reservations advised; credit cards not accepted.

Fish & Chips, 47 Endell Street, WC2.

ST. JAMES'S

Martinez, 25 Swallow Street, W1, tel. 734-4921. Authentically Spanish, and much frequented by prosperous Spaniards. Immaculate formal service and interesting food. Sherry bar and large 1920s dining room, both decorated with Spanish tiles. Prices moderate.

Wheeler's, 12a Duke of York Street, SW1, tel. 839-7137. Specializes in oysters and flatfish (Dover sole). Very small, intimate rooms. Reservations advised. Prices medium to high.

Colombina, 4–5 Duke of York Street, SW1, tel. 930-8279. Competent, with moderately priced Italian food.

Granary, 39 Albemarle Street, W1, tel. 493-2978. Self-service, busy, inexpensive and pleasant.

CHELSEA

Topolino D'Ischia, 5 Draycott Avenue, SW3, tel. 584-4003. Informal, good, fairly inexpensive Italian food.

Drake's, 2a Pond Place, SW3, tel. 584-4555. Air-conditioned and therefore by English standards rather posh. Good British cooking.

Victor's, 153 King's Road, SW3, tel. 352-0202. Imaginatively and assertively presented Italian food. Fixed, moderate price. No written menu; you have to ask.

Kennedy's, 316–18 King's Road, SW3. Lively atmosphere with good and inexpensive hamburgers eaten mainly by young people pleased to be in the King's Road. Open 11:00 A.M. to 1:00 A.M., seven days a week. A valuable place to know at times when most restaurants are closed, such as Sunday afternoons.

Johnny's Fish Bar, 494 King's Road, SW3. Highly praised fish and chips, to eat on or off the premises.

OFF YOUR ROUTE BUT EXCEPTIONAL VALUE

Modhiti's, 83 Bayham Street, NW1, tel. 485-7890 (Camden Town tube station). Unpromising exterior; lively, slightly bohemian middle-class clientele. Interesting Greek Cypriot food—almost embarrassingly inexpensive. Large tips are deserved.

Natraj, 93 Charlotte Street, W1, tel. 637-0050 (Goodge Street tube station). Nepalese food—a mild, creamy version of Indian.

Pubs

COVENT GARDEN

Lamb & Flag, 33 Rose Street, WC2. Ancient, dignified building and furnishings. Strong beer and good food, including a selection of cheeses and pâtés. For lunch, try to arrive before 12:30; the place soon fills with Covent Garden's media people.

Marquis of Anglesea, 39 Bow Street, WC2. Unpretentious and pleasant. A narrow choice of food, but fair value. The bar on the second story is often a peaceful place to eat.

Nag's Head, 10 James Street, WC2. Plusher than most Covent Garden pubs, with young, prosperous clientele.

INNS OF COURT

Princess Louise, 208 High Holborn, WC1. Magnificent antique woodwork. A delight for the connoisseur of bitter beer, with many of the fashionable English provincial brews. Men will find impressive stonework and metalwork in a surprising part of the building.

The George, 213 The Strand (corner of Devereux Court). Recommended for its special lunch section, towards the back of the bar.

Cheshire Cheese, 145 Fleet Street, EC4. Expensive and famous tourist trap. W. B. Yeats and friends discussed poetry here.

El Vino's, 47 Fleet Street, EC4. A meeting place for many of London's grander journalists. Women, curiously, are not served at the bar—in spite of legal action by feminists.

ST. JAMES'S

St. James's has few pubs, but two are good. They are both called The Red Lion. One is in Duke of York Street, SW1, with a very small but splendid Victorian interior. The other is in Crown Passage, SW1, and serves good pies at lunchtime.

CHELSEA

Markham Arms, (next to) 138 King's Road, SW3. Once dingy and half-forgotten, until colonized by Mary Quant and her friends. Now brassy and successful, with a fine exterior.

Queen's Elm, 241 Fulham Road (on corner of Old Church Street). Discreetly chic. Some of the wooden furnishings are rickety, others magnificent. Regular patrons very possessive.

King's Head and Eight Bells, 50 Cheyne Walk, SW3. Pleasant interior and famous lunches. Often crowded on weekends.

Cross Keys, Lawrence Street, SW3. More casual, but still with good lunches. Open fire in winter.

Black Lion, 35 Old Church Street, SW3. A decent substitute when The King's Head and Cross Keys are full.

Shops

COVENT GARDEN

Naturally British, 13 New Row, WC2, tel. 240-0551. Well-made toys and attractive household goods. Good for presents. Not cheap.

L. Cornelissen and Son, 22 Great Queen Street, WC2, tel. 405-3304. Etching and lithographic materials, and a rare selection of artists' pigments displayed in glittering rows of glass jars. Aims to preserve traditional techniques of painting; produces easels of eighteenth- and nineteenth-century design.

Arthur Middleton, 12 New Row, WC2, tel. 836-7042. Antique scientific instruments.

Philip Poole & Co., 182 Drury Lane, WC2, tel. 405-7097. Superb selection of calligraphers' nibs for sale—about five thousand types, most of them no longer made and some from before 1914. The shop is decorated with antique display cards of nibs from many countries. A delight.

Warehouse, 39 Neal Street, WC2, tel. 240-0931. Not a warehouse, but a small store devoted to loose beads and sequins.

Neal's Yard (half hidden in the triangle formed by Neal Street, Shorts Gardens and Monmouth Street). A delightful and placid courtyard, with a dovecote, and a dairy that sells sybaritic ice creams and cheeses.

The Kite Store, 69 Neal Street, WC2, tel. 836-1666. The name says it best.

Laura Ashley, 35–6 Bow Street, WC2, tel. 240-1997. Fine furnishings and dress fabrics.

CHELSEA

Chelsea has two antique markets—indoor bazaars with open-front booths. The atmosphere is informal. Bargains are hard to find but many stalls are a delight to look at. Antiquarius, 15 Flood Street (corner of Flood Street and King's Road), SW3, tel. 351-1145. Chelsea Antique Market, 245A King's Road, SW3, tel. 352-1425.

Laura Ashley, 157 Fulham Road, SW3, tel. 584-6939. Dresses. Other Laura Ashley shops are at 71 Lower Sloane Street, SW1, tel. 730-1771 (dress fabrics), and 40 Sloane Street, SW1, tel. 235-9728 (wallpaper and fabrics).

Index

Index

Index

Index